DEVON
Sketchbook

A pictorial guide to favourite places

Jim Watson

Thurlestone thatch

SURVIVAL BOOKS • BATH • ENGLAND

The hillside pathway, Lynmouth

Front cover illustration: Kingswear

First published 2014

All rights reserved. No part of this publication may be reproduced, stored in a retrieval system or recorded by any means, without prior written permission from the author

Text, illustrations and maps © Jim Watson 2014

Survival Books Limited
Office 169, 3 Edgar Buildings,
George Street, Bath BA1 2FJ, United Kingdom
Tel: +44 (0)1225-462135
email: sales@survivalbooks.net
website: www.survivalbooks.net

British Library Cataloguing in Publication Data
ACIP record for this book is available
from the British Library.
ISBN: 978-1-909282-70-4

Printed and bound in Malaysia by Tien Wah Press

CONTENTS

Introduction	5	South Devon	34	River Dart	68
North Devon	6	Seaton	36	Totnes	70
Lynton	8	Beer	38	Dartmoor	72
Lynmouth	10	Branscombe	40	Dartmoor Tour	73
Combe Martin	12	Sidmouth	42	Torcross	76
Exmoor	13	Budleigh Salterton	44	Slapton Sands	77
Exmoor Tour	13	Exmouth	46	Blackpool Sands	77
Exford	14	Topsham	48	Salcombe	78
Porlock	15	Dawlish	50	Prawle Point	81
Ilfracombe	16	Teignmouth	52	Kingsbridge	82
Mortehoe	20	Shaldon	54	Hope Cove	84
Woolacombe	21	Torquay	55	Thurlestone	86
Croyde	22	Cockington	57	Bigbury-on-Sea	88
Saunton Sands	23	Paignton	58	Plymouth	90
Barnstable	24	Brixham	60	Author's Notes	94
Bideford	28	Berry Head	63	Sketchbook series	96
Appledore	30	Dartmouth	64		
Clovelly	32	Kingswear	67		

Typical South Devon countryside on the edge of Dartmoor

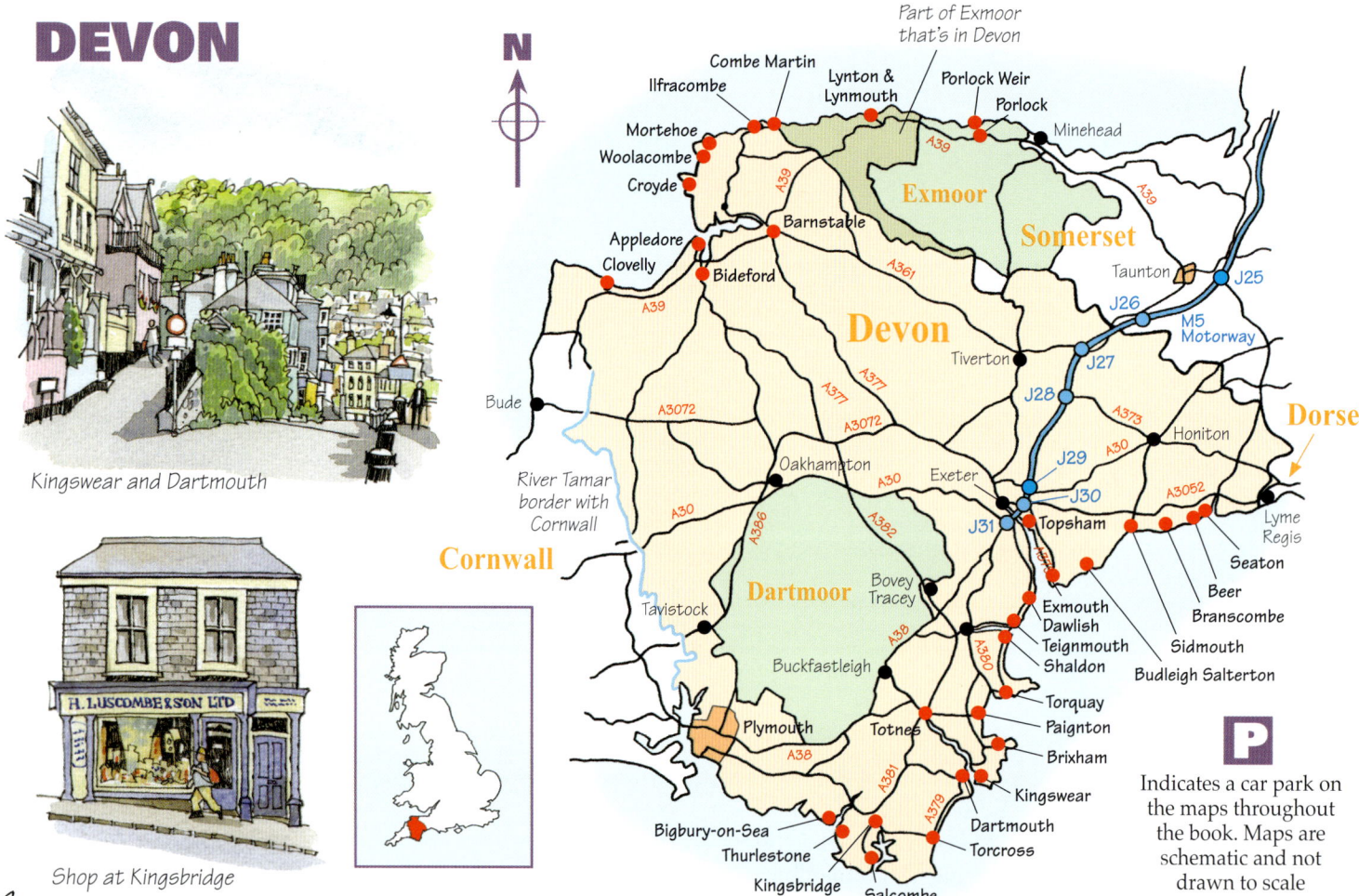

INTRODUCTION

Devon is many people's idea of the ideal country place to live. Given a big lottery win many of us would be heading for the West Country to spend it. A thatched cottage overlooking the sea. Wonderful!

But Devon is far more than a country idyll set in an equable climate. It's certainly an outdoor kind of a region. Whatever you like to do outdoors you'll probably find all you need here. Some counties are pleased to boast one National Park, but Devon contains two, all of Dartmoor and a significant piece of Exmoor.

Unique in England, the county boasts two separate and distinct coastlines, with some of the best beaches in the southwest. You can tramp across wild moorland, walk along the South West Coast Path and explore the oldest part of the geological treasure house, the Jurassic Coast. Devon also has some of Britain's most-loved seaside resorts, historic towns and cities; picturesque villages set in gentle hedged landscapes crossed by narrow winding roads; and some of the best sailing and boating centres in the southwest. Truly, it has something for everybody.

I've been visiting and enjoying Devon for well over 40 years and researching this book has enabled me to renew my acquaintance with old friends and to discover new places that I look forward to visiting again. Most of my favourites were much the same as I remember them. Devon has a timelessness that's reassuring and comforting, especially if you live in a part of the country that's rapidly changing.

This book will guide you to a wealth of favourite places along the north and south coasts of Devon, plus some in the Exmoor and Dartmoor National Parks. It will tell you how you can drive there, where you can park and what to look out for. I also hope it informs, entertains and, if you're a visitor, gives you something to enjoy when you're back home.

What it can't do is provide the unexpected surprise that can stay with you forever. I've enjoyed many on my travels throughout this remarkable county. I hope you will too.

Jim Watson
Rugby, 2014

The Anchor inn, Beer

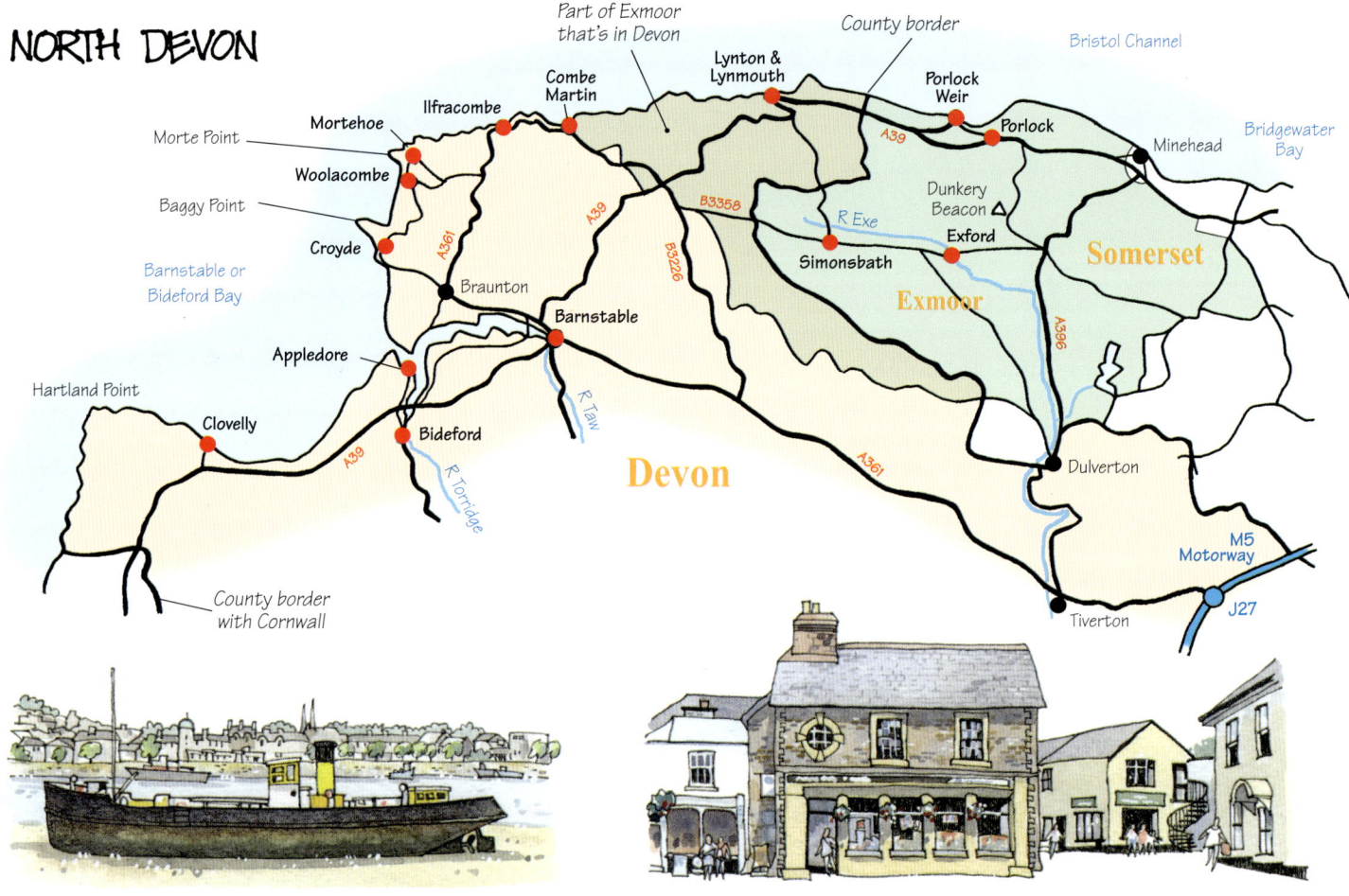

The M5 motorway and the A30 trunk road slice Devon in two along a thinly populated swathe of small settlements, which emphasis the division and effectively turns one county into two.

   North Devon is less touristy than the south, with an unspoilt and unsophisticated charm, a place of few dual carriageways and no railway beyond Minehead; of quiet pastoral delights; forest walks and relaxed drinks in real country pubs.

   There is excitement too: dramatic cliffs – some of the highest in England; the western beaches washed by Atlantic rollers; smooth green hills slashed by deep and mysterious wooded combes; and dear old Exmoor, more approachable, more colourful and less crowded than Dartmoor.

The Black Venus Inn at Challacombe

The beach at Porlock Weir
(Actually in Somerset, not Devon, but far too good to miss)

7

LYNTON

Set on a wooded cliff top 500ft (150m) above its sister resort of Lynmouth, Lynton's popularity soared in the 1890s with the publication of *Lorna Doone* and the arrival of literary tourists in search of the book's romantic settings. The summer invasion continues but the town manages to retain an attractive gentility largely unsullied by the excesses of modern tourism.

The imposing Town Hall on Lee Road epitomises Victorian-Edwardian values. It was the gift of publisher George Newnes, a frequent visitor to the town who also financed the nearby cliff railway.

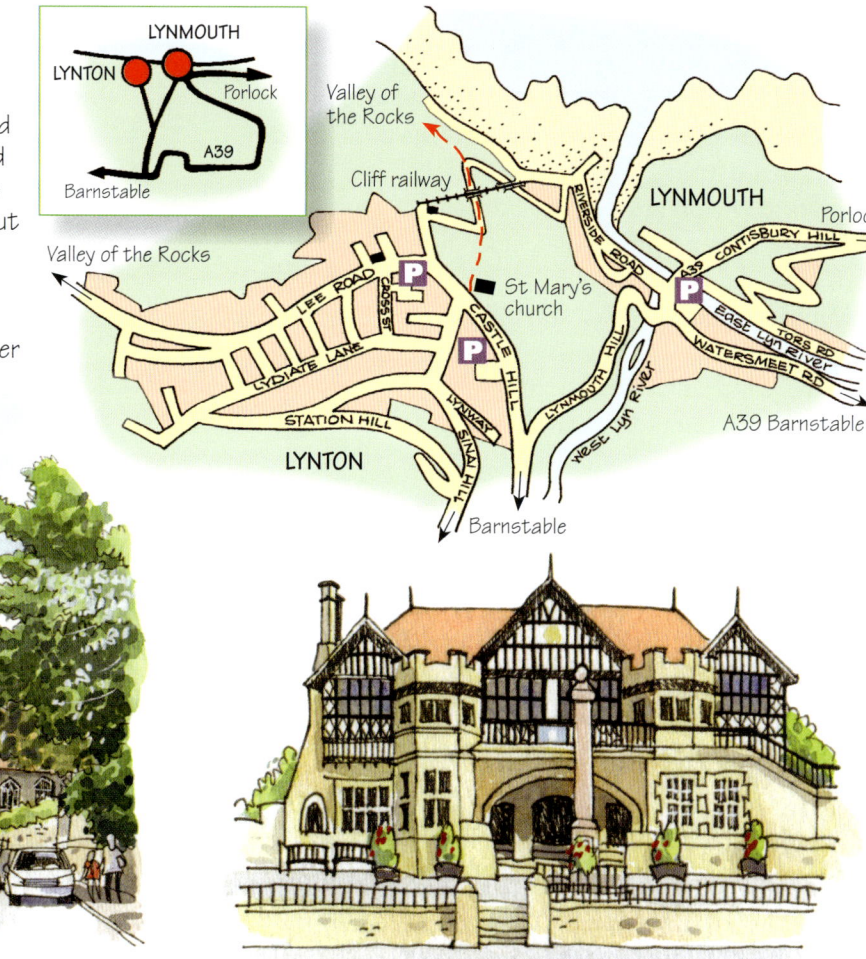

Lee Road

The Town Hall

Queen Street

Beginning at St Mary's church, a tarmac path takes you a mile or so west of Lynton into the Valley of Rocks, a dry heathland valley probably formed during the ice age. It's dominated by extraordinary rock formations jutting from the grassy floor that have been given fanciful names such as The Devil's Cheesewring and Ragged Jack. There's a car park in the valley but it's most impressive when approached on foot.

You may be lucky enough to spot the valley's famous feral goats that have run wild here for, it's said, over a thousand years. More recently they have been accused of running a bit too wild and going on the rampage, munching on flower beds, raiding washing lines and allegedly destroying the village cricket pitch. So in a cunning plan to curb their numbers Lynton Town Council announced in 2013 that 80% of the female goats would be given contraceptive injections – if the villagers could raise the £12,000 cost. See 'em while you can.

Lynton's main shopping area winds along Lee Road into Castle Hill. Little alleys lead off with some attractive gift shops. There's even a cinema, up an alley next to the town hall.

This is prime walking country, not just along the coastal path but inland too. Watersmeet, one of the area's most celebrated beauty spots, is appropriately set where two rivers meet in a magnificent wooded gorge, a couple of miles east of the town.

A feral goat

The Valley of the Rocks

LYNMOUTH

Prettier and more of a village than its cliff top neighbour, the beauty and romance of Lynmouth has been celebrated by artists and writers alike. Gainsborough was a fan, Shelley spent his honeymoon here and R.D. Blackmore, the author of *Lorna Doone* stayed in Mars Hill, the oldest part of the village.

The perfection was shattered on August 15, 1952, after nine inches (23cm) of rain fell on Exmoor in 24 hours. Floodwater surged down the valley, hundreds of trees were uprooted, all the bridges were swept away, Lynmouth harbour was destroyed, houses were demolished and 34 people were killed.

Reminders of the terrible devastation still remain around the village and it's vividly recalled in the Flood Memorial Hall by the harbour. Though few houses were rebuilt, the river was diverted away from the village and the harbour redesigned. Even the Rhenish Tower, a 19th-century folly built on the harbour wall to provide seawater for bathers, was faithfully recreated.

With a street full of gift and tea shops clustered around the harbour and a large coach park at its head, Lynmouth has become more touristy, but still has undeniable charm. And the view of the village from along the harbour wall is perfection.

Lynmouth harbour and village

Rhenish Tower

Cliff railway

The cliff railway

The much photographed scene of whitewashed houses and the 14th-century thatched Rising Sun Inn climbing up the wooded hill from Riverside Road will be familiar to anyone with a Devon calendar or a postcard from Lynton and Lynmouth. Even so the sight of the real thing can be a considerable pleasure.

Lynmouth beach is a mixture of sand and shingle. Pleasant enough, but unspectacular.

Opened in 1890, a remarkable cliff railway driven by an ingenious counter-balance system links Lynmouth with Lynton 500ft (150m) above. Connected by a steel cable, one car goes up the steep 1 in 1.75 gradient as the other descends. Traction is created by putting the two cars out of balance using the weight of 700 gallons of water pumped into the top car's tank and emptying it when it reaches the bottom

Riding the cars is an essential part of the Lynton and Lynmouth visitor experience, but if you prefer to walk up or down the cliff, a tarmac path zig-zags through woodland alongside the railway.

Riverside Road & The Rising Sun Inn

COMBE MARTIN

Set at the end of a sheltered valley, Combe Martin is famous for its unfeasibly long main street which straggles for around two miles down to the seafront. Even driving along it seems to take forever.

The beach is a mixture of sand and rock set in a small rocky bay, a decent place to swim with plenty of pools to poke about in at low tide. This stretch of coastline is fearsomely spectacular and boasts some of the highest cliffs in Britain. It's well-worth exploring – with care!

The Pack o' Cards Inn on Combe Martin High Street was reputedly built by an 18th-century gambler with his winnings. The oddity originally had 52 windows (some were later boarded up), four stories representing the suits and thirteen doors on each level for the number of cards in each suit.

EXMOOR

Once a royal hunting forest, Exmoor was designated a National Park in 1954. It's one of the country's smallest, covering 267 square miles with 29% of it in Devon and 71% in Somerset.

The scenery in the park is amazingly varied: high cliffs and plunging ravines; fast-flowing rivers; wooded valleys; picturesque villages; and a high plateau of open heathland with sensational views across the Bristol Channel to Wales.

Though managed by the National Park Authority, much of Exmoor is still privately owned and farmed but there's still good access to a wide network of bridleways and footpaths.

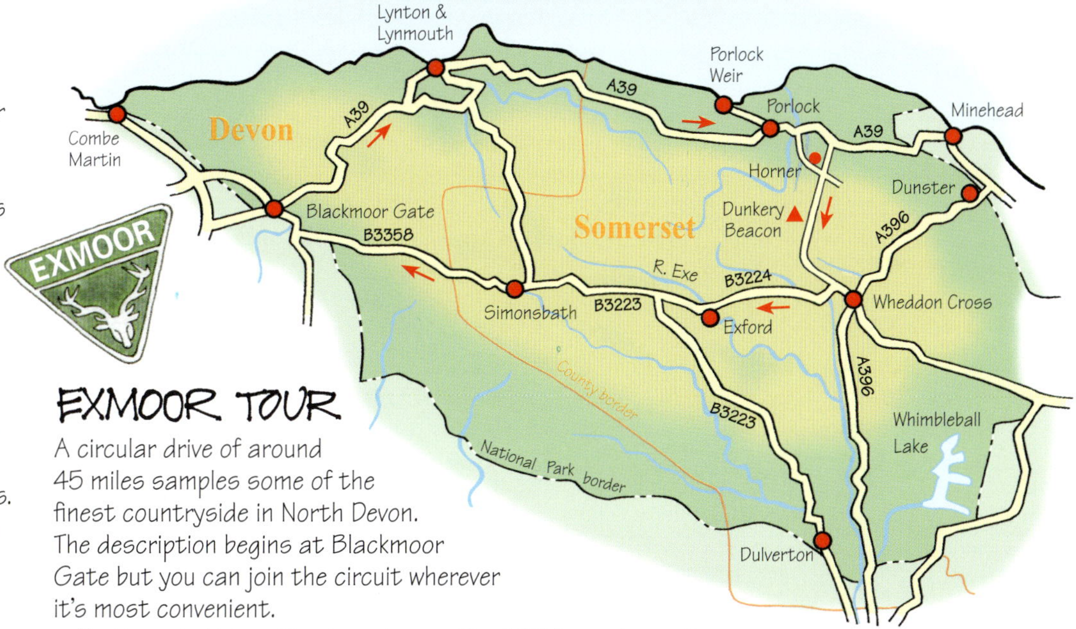

EXMOOR TOUR

A circular drive of around 45 miles samples some of the finest countryside in North Devon. The description begins at Blackmoor Gate but you can join the circuit wherever it's most convenient.

On the outskirts of Lynton stay on the A39 for a dramatic ride along a wooded ravine before emerging at Lynmouth. Beyond the village, pause to admire the views from a hillside car park just after a cattle grid. Approaching Porlock there's a choice of routes: a scenic toll road zig-zagging through woodland or down the famous 1 in 4 Porlock Hill. After visiting Porlock Weir rejoin the A39 towards Minehead, then after a half mile or so turn right onto a narrow road signed Horner & Luccombe.

About half a mile beyond the fairy-tale hamlet of Horner, turn right into a narrow wooded road signed Dunkery Beacon. Climb steadily for a couple of miles and emerge from the woods onto high heathland. The beacon, at 1,704ft (518m) Exmoor's highest point, is a short walk from a car park. Resume on the minor road and gradually descend to join the B3224 near Wheddon Cross. Continue on to Exford and Simonsbath and rejoin the A39 at Blackmoor Gate.

The Exmoor Forest Inn at Simonsbath

EXFORD

Regarded as the centre of Exmoor, Exford is an attractive no-nonsense village with an absence of twee country cottages but with a strong sense of community. An ancient crossing of the River Exe, the present substantial stone bridge was built in 1930.

The main street winds sleepily past a large village green and shops providing the necessities for life in a fairly remote country area. There's a post office and general store, a garage, an agricultural machinery supplier and an amazing shop packed with all manner of outdoor clothes, hats, walking sticks, horse saddles and tack – all in various shades of green and brown. None of your dayglow cagoules here, frightening the wildlife.

Exford also has two hotels. The White Horse Inn beside the river is headquarters of the Devon & Somerset Staghounds which has hunted on Exmoor since 1875. It's a good place to stop for refreshment but if you have strong views on hunting this is probably not the place to air them!

Exford

The view north from Dunkery Beacon

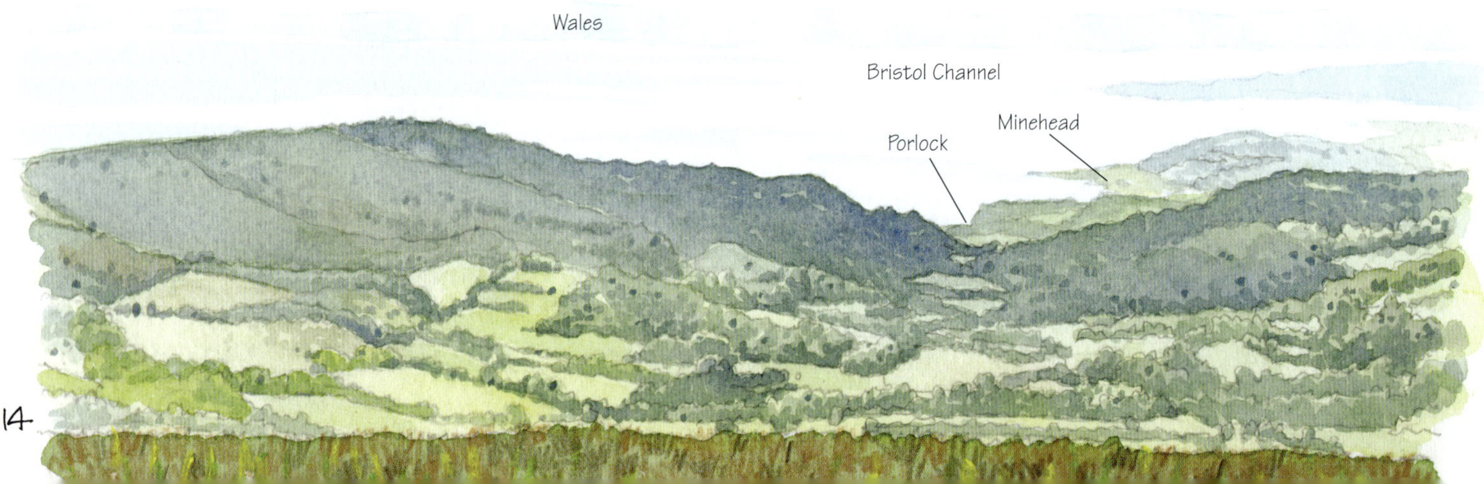

PORLOCK

Porlock High Street

Porlock has everything a visitor could want, except perhaps the sea. However, this is taken care of a couple of miles away at the ancient and atmospheric harbour of Porlock Weir, once a busy port for trade with South Wales.

Today it's a sleepy spot with thatched cottages, a rambling old inn, a restaurant and a handful of gift shops. The beach isn't your golden sand variety but even more impressive; a wide bank of smooth pink, blue and grey duck egg-sized stones, difficult to walk on but beautiful to behold. Weather-beaten groynes totter down to the shoreline and boats scatter all over the place at low tide. Backed by wooded hills, it's an artist's paradise.

Porlock lies in the Somerset part of the Exmoor National Park, beautifully situated in a deep hollow, overlooked on three sides by hogbacked Hills. The High Street winds attractively past hotels, cafés, a 13th-century church, antique shops, galleries and an excellent food store.

The late 18th-century poets Wordsworth and Coleridge roamed these hills, with Coleridge complaining that he was interrupted by 'a man from Porlock' while writing *Kubla Khan* and was unable to finish it. Another poet friend, Robert Southey, stayed at The Ship Inn which features prominently in *Lorna Doone*.

Modern-day visitors can park at the village hall at the western end of the High Street or in a car park at the other end, near the Exmoor Classic Cars Museum.

Porlock Weir

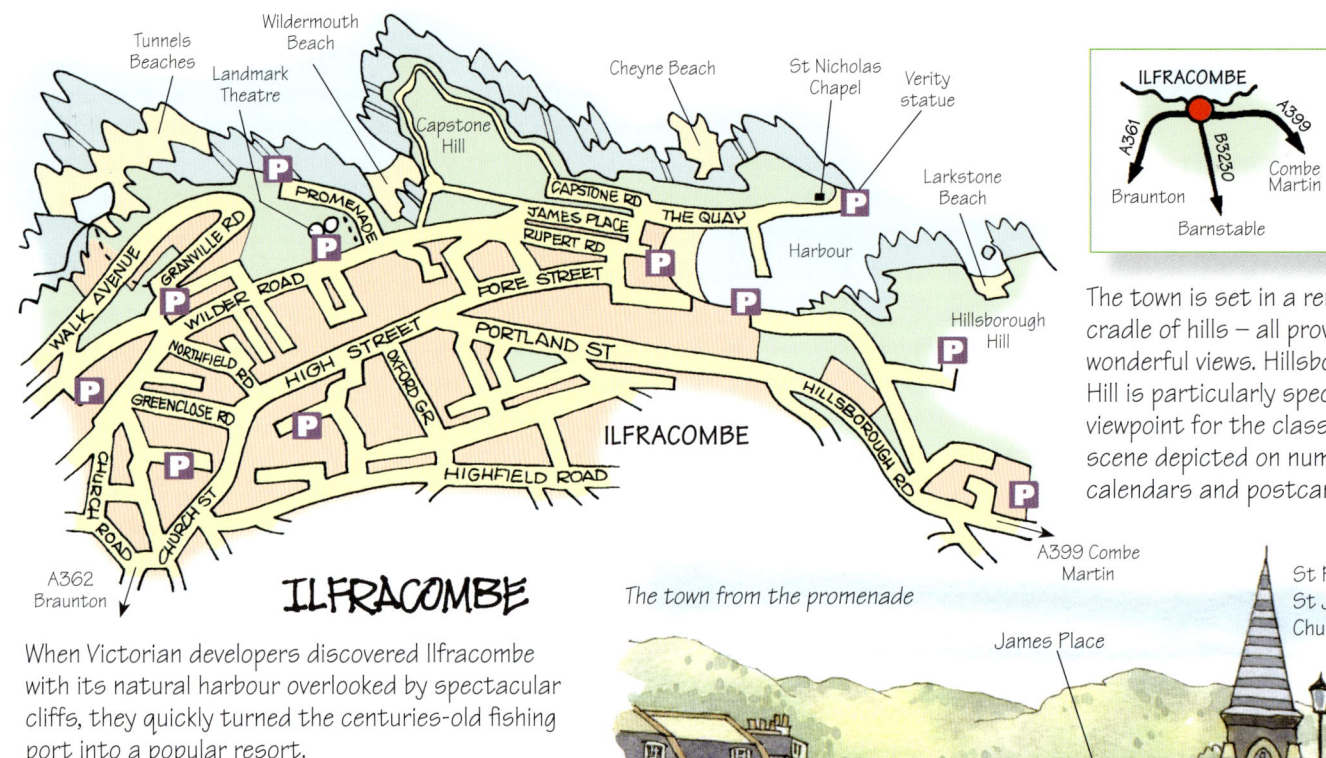

ILFRACOMBE

The town is set in a remarkable cradle of hills – all providing wonderful views. Hillsborough Hill is particularly special as the viewpoint for the classic harbour scene depicted on numerous calendars and postcards.

The town from the promenade

When Victorian developers discovered Ilfracombe with its natural harbour overlooked by spectacular cliffs, they quickly turned the centuries-old fishing port into a popular resort.

These days the elegant Victorian and Regency terraces and villas on the hillside look a bit jaded but there's a enough going on to maintain the town's position as the top resort in north Devon.

Fishing, mainly for crab and lobster, continues, with a small fleet of brightly-painted boats moored on the south side of the harbour.

Five of Ilfracombe's six beaches are sand and shingle with rock pools at low tide. The other beach – actually a series of little coves – is also the oddest. Tunnels Beaches are accessed from Northfield Road through tunnels bored by Welsh miners in the 19th century. Previously inaccessible, the beaches are of grey sand and shingle towered over by grey cliffs creating a slightly claustrophobic moonscape. But not in a bad way, couples even get married here. Privately owned, the beach area is being developed with bars and cafes. Worth the small entrance fee – you'll never see anything like it.

A tarmac walkway follows the shoreline around the base of Capstone Hill providing some sensational views of the remarkable ragged and jagged rock formations along the way. A walk to the grassy hilltop is rewarded with a wider view, even – if you're lucky – a glimpse of the Welsh coast across the Bristol Channel and Lundy Island, 25 miles out to sea where the Bristol Channel meets the Atlantic Ocean.

Fore Street

Running steeply down to the harbour, Fore Street has an eclectic mix of gift shops, restaurants and pubs, including the 14th-century George and Dragon Inn and the old police station, now the La Gendarmerie restaurant.

The coastline from Capstone Hill

St Nicholas Chapel

Rear of Capstone Crescent

Hillsborough Hill

Cheyne Beach

A pathway climbs around Lantern Hill to St Nicholas Chapel, the town's oldest building which once offered succor to 14th-century pilgrims en route to Hartland Abbey. It later served as a lighthouse for over 500 years and a family dwelling for two parents and 14 children.

The aptly-named Landmark Theatre, reminiscent of a pair of massive white binoculars, is a £4.5 million arts and entertainment complex completed in 1997 as part of the council's regeneration plan. The twin cones, each 73ft (22.5m) high were built using more than 300,000 bricks.

Nearby is an interesting mosaic marking out the world triple jump record of over 16ft (18.29m) achieved by former Ilfracombe resident Jonathen Edwards in the 1995 World Athletic Championships. It does look a remarkably long stretch. Children and adults who really shouldn't, cannot resist trying to emulate his jump. Most get no further than the 'hop' section.

Jubilee Gardens are a glorious celebration of the Victorian legacy, where you can sit and admire a wonderful panorama of the town and the hills beyond.

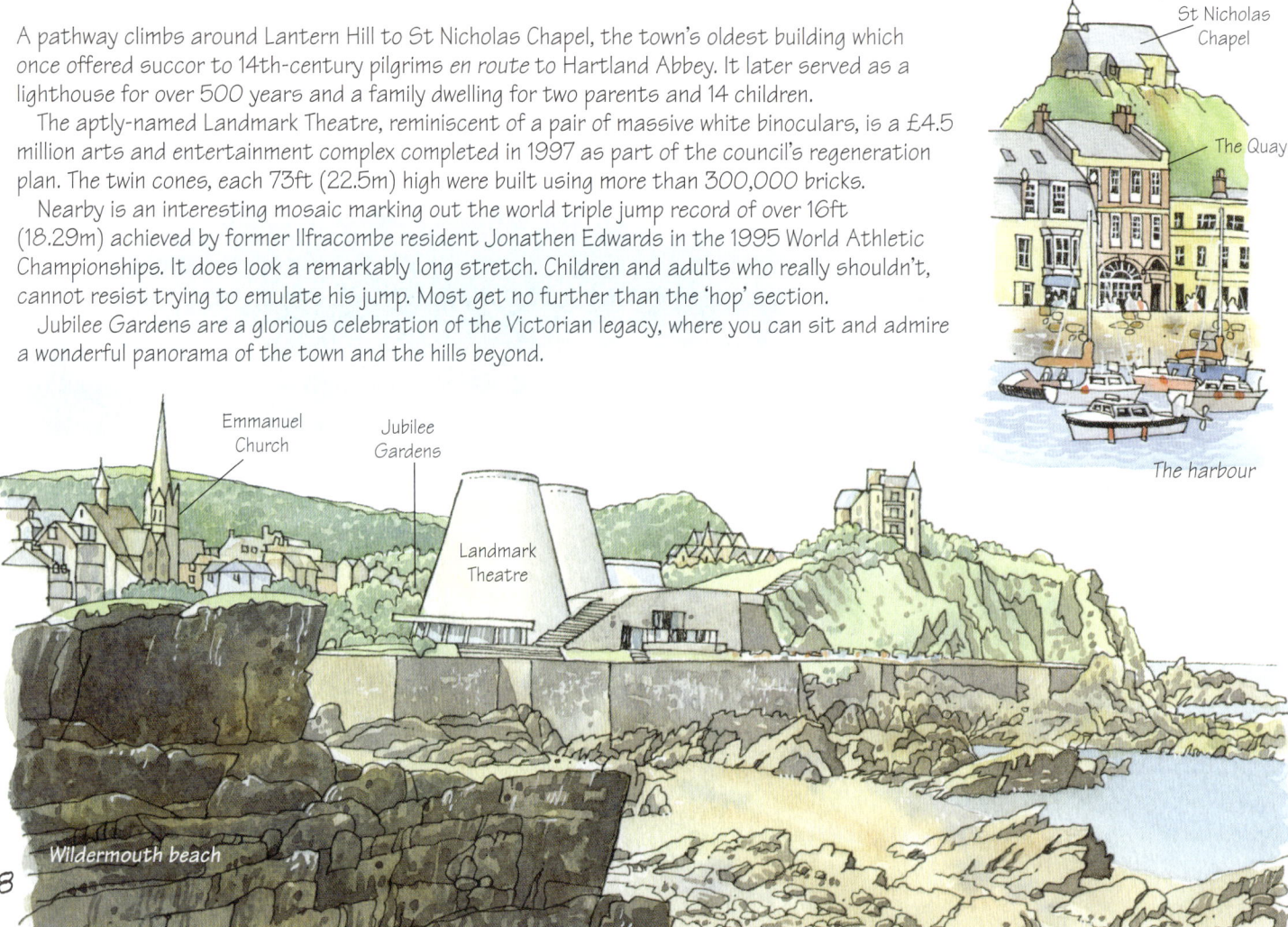

St Nicholas Chapel

The Quay

The harbour

Emmanuel Church

Jubilee Gardens

Landmark Theatre

Wildermouth beach

Fast food outlets and gift shops line the harbourside with The Quay, a century-old inn turned into a modish restaurant and bar by contemporary artist and co-owner Damien Hirst, providing a more upmarket experience.

Summer visitors who'd like to sample a quieter pace of life can board the MS *Oldenburg* for a trip to Lundy Island.

An Ilfracombe fishing boat

Damien Hirst has invested heavily and generously in the area but his most controversial gift to the town has undoubtedly been *Verity*, a 66ft (20m) bronze-clad statue of a pregnant woman holding a sword aloft while standing on a base of legal books and holding the scales of justice.

Hoisted into position beside the harbour car park on October 16, 2012, the statue has received a 'mixed' reception. Whatever you think of modern art and this piece in particular, you can't miss it. And like it or loathe it, Hirst has loaned *Verity* to North Devon council until 2032.

The Lundy ferry

Verity

MORTEHOE

Mentioned in the Domesday Book and formerly a small farming community, the village of Mortehoe has grown to cater for modern tourism. A large car park and a vast caravan and camping site on the outskirts bear testament to the area's popularity. There's also three pubs, a village store, post office, restaurants and cafes.

The Heritage Museum behind the car park revels in the swashbuckling history of local smuggling and shipwrecks. Walk a mile out of the village to Morte Point to see the sharp-rocked scene of the crimes and possibly the seals which bask on the north side.

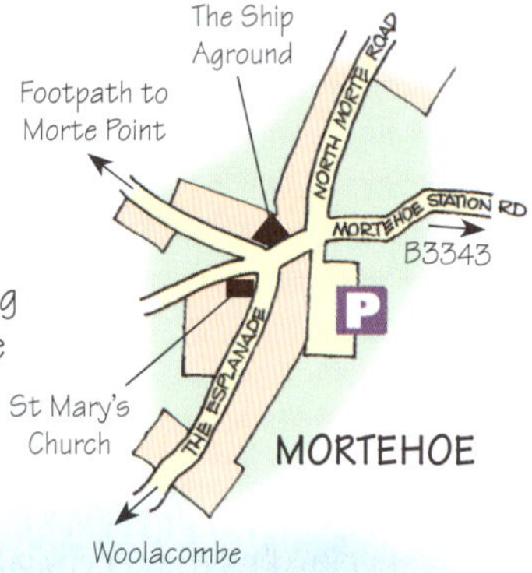

St Mary's Church The oldest parts date back to Norman times. The bell tower, carved pews and the chest tomb of a former incumbent, Sir William de Tracy, are medieval.

The rugged north coast of Devon turns sharply south at Mortehoe to a long stretch of the best beaches in the county. Only the great rocky outcrop of Baggy Point and the broad slash of the rivers Taw and Torridge estuaries interrupt this 10 miles of continuous sandy delight.

The Ship Aground Inn

Mortehoe village centre

WOOLACOMBE

Driving south along the cramped road from Mortehoe a elevated view of the sea opens up on your right and you think nothing can beat this. Then something does. You turn a corner into Woolacombe and a vast golden expanse of super-clean beach is revealed. The rather characterless village cannot compete but it doesn't need to. Woolacombe is all about the beach, the village is only there to provide facilities for the droves of summer visitors.

The resort became popular in the late 19th century. A few seafront Regency villas remain but it's now dominated by hotels, caravan sites, holiday homes, restaurants and cafés. Lively in summer but rather sad in winter. Except of course for that beach!

During the Second World War, small boat crews and infantry of the US Army practised amphibious landing assaults here in preparation for the Invasion of Normandy, part of Operation Overlord. Woolacombe's long flat beach was considered to closely resemble the one at Omaha. A stone memorial to the soldiers, dedicated in 1992, is sited on the grassy headland at the northern end of the beach.

CROYDE

Blessed with a beautiful crescent bay and acres of golden sand, Croyde attracts a multitude of summer beach-lovers and surfing devotees all year round. However, away from the beach hot-spots and the Moor Lane camp sites, Croyde is also a pretty village of thatched cottages and narrow lanes, although it can be horrendously busy, especially when there's a beach music festival taking place and youth culture is at full blast.

The Thatch – a surfer's hangout in Croyde village

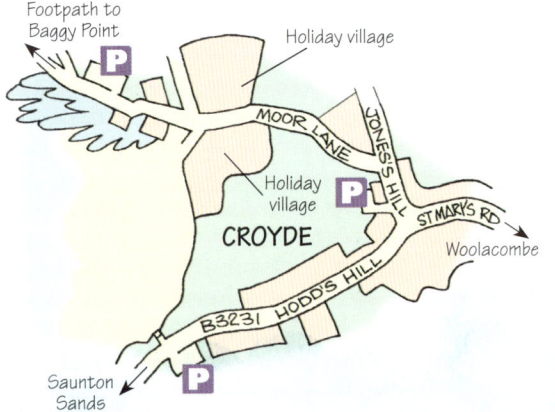

Thatched cottage at the centre of Croyde

The village hall car park fills up quickly but there are two others serving the beach. The Moor Lane end is the livelier with fast food eateries and beach shops. For a quieter time head for the one at Hood's Hill, but you'll have to cart all your gear down a long flight of steps to the beach.

Croyde beach

Baggy Point

A lovely mile-long walk out of Croyde, Baggy Point is a fantastic viewpoint. The vertical cliffs attract rock climbers and from September to November hordes of nesting birds.

SAUNTON SANDS

The road from Croyde climbs to an elevated view across the area's largest beach of all, Saunton Sands. With the Torridge and Torr estuary three miles distant and Atlantic breakers endlessly rolling in, it's a magnificent sight. Less developed for long stay holidays than Woolacombe, Saunton Sands caters more for day visitors with a car park, toilets and café at the northern end and the white 1930s Saunton Sands Hotel on the clifftop above. Good for bathing, although the southern end should be avoided due to strong and unpredictable currents in the estuary.

Not only a world class family beach, Saunton is also renowned for some of the best surf in the country. When there's a good swell it can produce line after line of beautiful long slow rollers that are an irresistible draw for longboarders from all over the country.

And that's not all. Between the beach and Braunton village lies Braunton Burrows, one of the largest sand dune systems in England, famous for its plant and animal life which received Biosphere status from UNESCO in 2002. It's home to a huge variety of moths and butterflies. Flocks of wading birds populate the estuary and migrating birds use it as a resting place.

Saunton Sands

BARNSTAPLE

North Devon's largest town and local government centre, Barnstaple grew up around the lowest crossing point of the River Taw about seven miles upstream of its outlet into the Bristol Channel. The major part of the town sits on the eastern bank connected to the western by the ancient 16-arch Long Bridge.

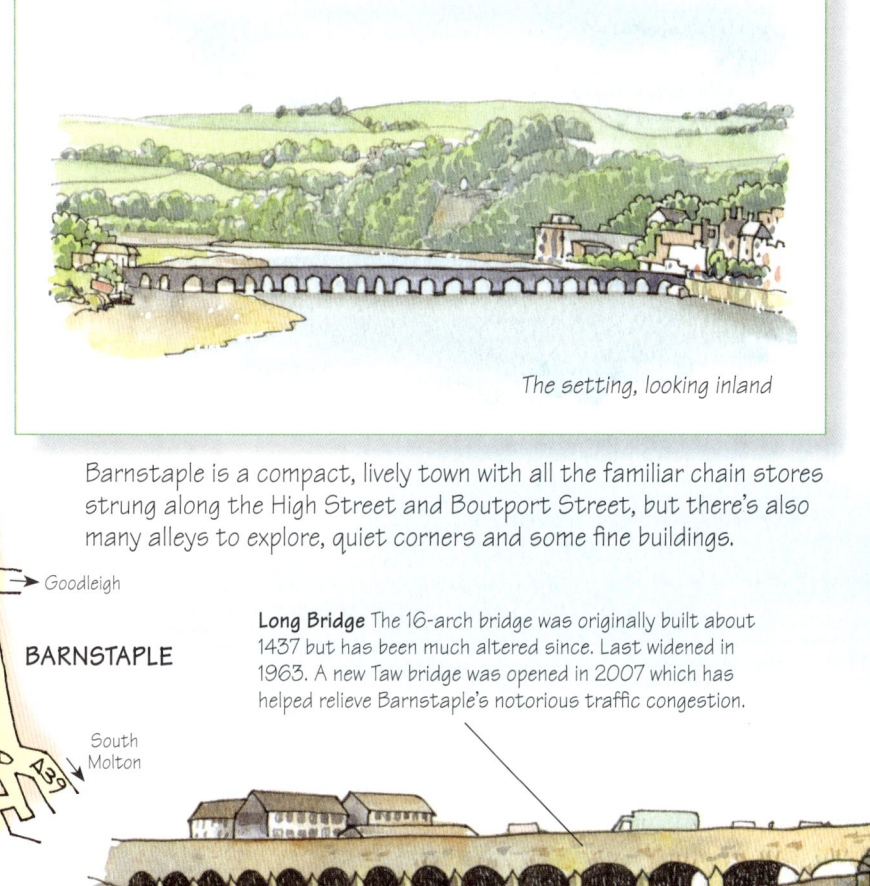

The setting, looking inland

Barnstaple is a compact, lively town with all the familiar chain stores strung along the High Street and Boutport Street, but there's also many alleys to explore, quiet corners and some fine buildings.

Long Bridge The 16-arch bridge was originally built about 1437 but has been much altered since. Last widened in 1963. A new Taw bridge was opened in 2007 which has helped relieve Barnstaple's notorious traffic congestion.

The historic Guildhall & High Street

The town's early prosperity was built on wool, much of it exported, but when the River Taw began to silt up business transferred to Bideford. Some sea-going trade survived and even today coastal vessels still dock with building materials and other bulk cargoes. Clay dug from the Taw and Torridge estuary sustained an important pottery industry in the area for hundreds of years.

The Georgian Guildhall, built 1826, has been central to Barnstable's history over the last two centuries. It's still used by the Town Council and tours are available to view the old courtroom, mayor's parlour and town plate.

The **Museum of North Devon** has lively and imaginative exhibits with Tarka the Otter featuring heavily. The Tarka Trail passes through the town

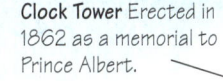
Boutport Street

Clock Tower Erected in 1862 as a memorial to Prince Albert.

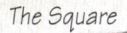
The Square

St Peter's church

Already the commercial centre for North Devon, Barnstaple was first granted a charter in AD930. Demands for health regulation of food in Victorian times resulted in a covered Pannier Market being opened behind the Guildhall in 1855. The iconic iron-pillared building with its glass and timber roof is little changed since. Over a hundred yards long, it houses traditional, craft and antique markets plus the sale of fruit, vegetables, dairy products antiques clothes and books. No visitor to Barnstaple should miss it.

Butchers Row runs alongside, built of Bath Stone with 33 archways and a canopy to provide shade from the sun, originally to accommodate butcher's shops. A few remain but now it's largely locally-sourced food shops and cafés.

St Peter's parish church is interesting for its large collection of monuments and a novel broach spire, twisted and warped by time and temperature.

Pannier Market

Butcher's Row

Butcher's Row

Barnstaple became a major port for trade with America, managed locally at Queen Anne's Walk. Completed in 1713, the ornate building by the river now houses the Barnstaple Heritage Centre. Under the statue of Queen Anne is the Tome Stone, where bargains and deals were struck in front of witnesses. The area in front of the Walk was the site of 'The Great Quay' in Elizabethan times.

Queen Anne's Walk

Bar in Boutport Street

The Royal & Fortesque Hotel and the Bank café, bar & bistro

BIDEFORD

Spread along the west bank of the River Torridge, the small town of Bideford has a long history as a port and market town. East-of-the-Water, on the opposite side of the river, is a good place to spot remnants of the old shipbuilding industry, and admire the ancient boats being renovated by nautical enthusiasts.

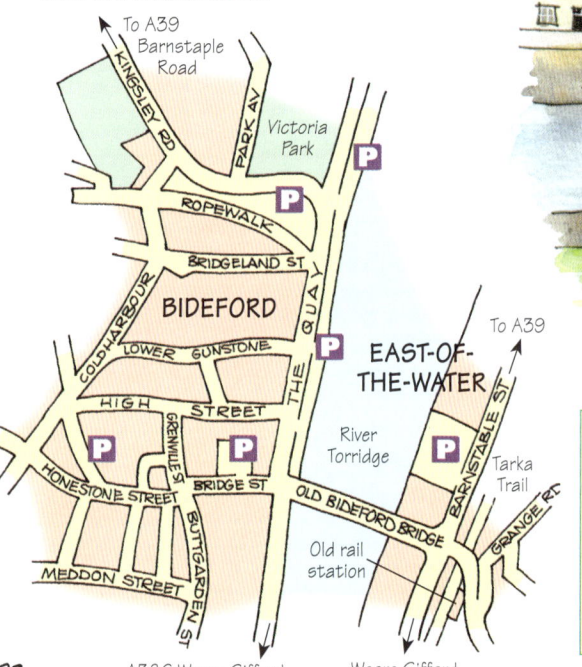

Bideford from East-of-the-Water

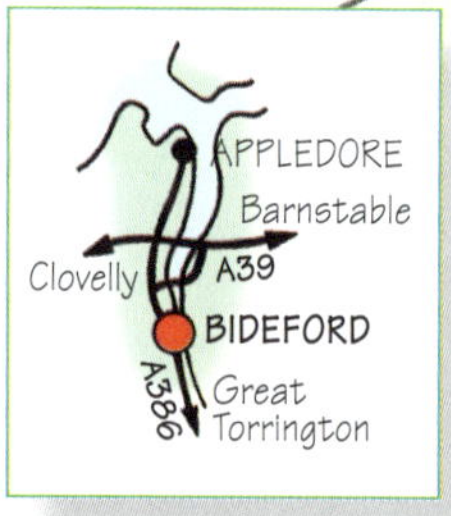

The Long Bridge straddles the broad expanse of the Torridge, first built around 1286 and reconstructed in stone in 1474. It's been regularly reinforced and widened since then with the result that no two of the bridge's 24 arches have the same span. Two arches collapsed in 1968 causing traffic chaos. The crossing was finally augmented in 1987 by the Torridge Bridge, a high sweep of modern concrete a mile downstream.

Refreshingly untouristy, Bideford rises steeply from the quay, its sloping narrow streets and alleys lined with traditional 'butcher, baker and greengrocer' shops alongside more modern craft outlets, galleries and antique stores. The traffic free lanes and the tree-lined quayside with its open aspect are particularly pleasant to wander around. Guns captured from the Spanish Armada in 1588 are displayed in Victoria Park at the northern end of the quay. There's a smaller version of Barnstaple's Pannier Market in Market Place, built in 1884, though a market has been held here since 1272.

Across the Long Bridge in East-of-the-Water the disused rail station, closed by Beeching in 1965, survives as a atmospheric tea room with the Tarka Trail, a 180-mile cycle and pedestrian way, running along the route of the track.

The Quay and the Torridge Bridge

The Katherine & May at Brunswick Wharf, Bideford

Bideford has a proud maritime history. From Norman times until the 18th-century the port was the property of the Granville family. Sir Richard Granville commanded the ships that carried the first settlers to Virginia and later took part in the defeat of the Spanish Armada in 1588. Sir Walter Raleigh is reputed to have landed the first shipment of tobacco in Bideford.

Shipbuilding flourished here during the 18th and 19th centuries but began to decline in the 1890s as shipyards began to build steel ships.

A historic tall ship, Kathleen & May, built during 1900 in Flintshire, is registered at Bideford and can often be seen moored in the Torridge. The only wooden triple-masted sailing schooner still in existence, she regularly sails across the Bristol Channel and the Irish Sea.

APPLEDORE

The quaint old port of Appledore occupies an integral position at the junction of the rivers Torr and Torridge before they flow out to sea. This is home to England's last purely commercial shipbuilder, one of the few North Devon industries that does not depend on tourism.

Fisherman's cottages, some dating back to the Elizabethan era, line the narrow streets, climbing up the hillside from the long quayside where there's fine views across the Torridge estuary to Instow and the hills beyond.

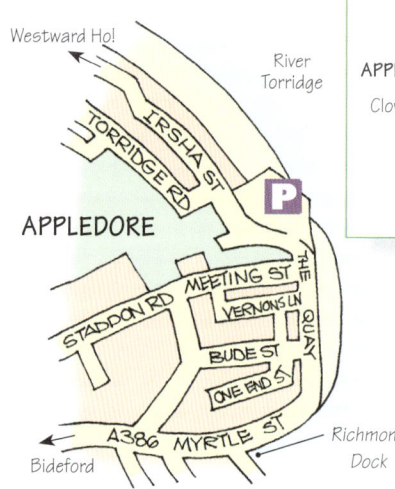
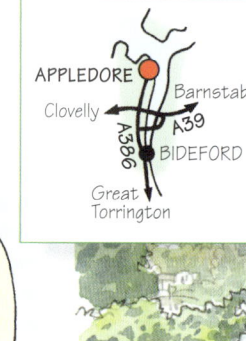

The beach is sandy and bathing safe – provided you aren't too ambitious. This is an estuary with strong currents.

Shops are the traditional variety and there's plenty of tempting cobbled courtyards, alleys and corners to explore.

Look out for a Hosking's ice cream van. This creamy delight has been made in Appledore since 1936 and is sold only from its 14 vans throughout North Devon.

House in Meeting Street

Former Independent Chapel built 1820. Now converted into a single dwelling called Bell Tower House.

Meeting Street

Until the mid 19th century the Appledore riverbank was crowded with boat builders and ship repair yards which are now all closed, the last boatyard being redeveloped for housing in the 1990s.

Shipbuilding today is limited to the Appledore Shipbuilders Yard which, when completed in 1970 just up the river at Bidna Marsh, was the largest covered dry dock in Europe. After it opened, the Richmond Dock, a shipbuilding and repair site at the southern end of Appledore quay, largely fell into disuse. When it first opened In 1855, the Richmond Dock was the largest dry dock in the Bristol Channel.

A period of uncertainty followed but, after a local campaign, the Richmond Dock was finally reopened in 2012 for the decommissioning and dismantling of vessels.

Schoolroom of the Appledore Baptist Chapel, built in 1897

The war memorial, Churchfield Road

Irsha Street

Appledore's colour-washed houses are a delight. Partly-cobbled Irsha Street is a particularly fine example, winding through much of the northern end of town and only just wide enough in places for a single car.

31

CLOVELLY

North Devon's superstar, set-piece visitor attraction, Clovelly is almost impossibly picturesque, yet still manages to hang on to reality and is home to around 450 real people, thanks to the astute management of the Hamlyn family who have owned the estate since 1738. The village is traffic-free, second homes are banned, hotels and B&Bs restricted. White, flower-decked cottages line the cobbled main street as it plunges steeply some 400ft (122m) over a half mile. Battered sledges are used for transporting goods. The donkeys that used to haul them are now retired, though some are still brought out for children to pat.

Crazy Kate's Cottage The oldest cottage in Clovelly. Named after a fisherman's widow.

Temple Bar Cottage The street passes underneath the kitchen and dining room of the cottage

Red Lion Hotel

Lifeboat House

Clovelly

Red Lion Hotel & the harbour

Main Street

The stony beach with its tiny harbour and chunky 14th-century jetty is a good place to look back and appreciate the village's magnificent setting, deep in a cleft beneath towering wooded cliffs. It's a long climb back up the main street but you can take a Land Rover taxi back to the car park which leave Red Lion Hotel every fifteen minutes or so.

Maintenance costs on scenic splendour are high and there's an entrance fee to pay as you pass through the large car park and visitor centre at the top of the hill.

All visitors to North Devon should visit Clovelly at least once but if the crowds and contrived tweeness of the village are too much for you, try nearby Buck Mills, which is similar but smaller than its grand neighbour. There's also a free car park!

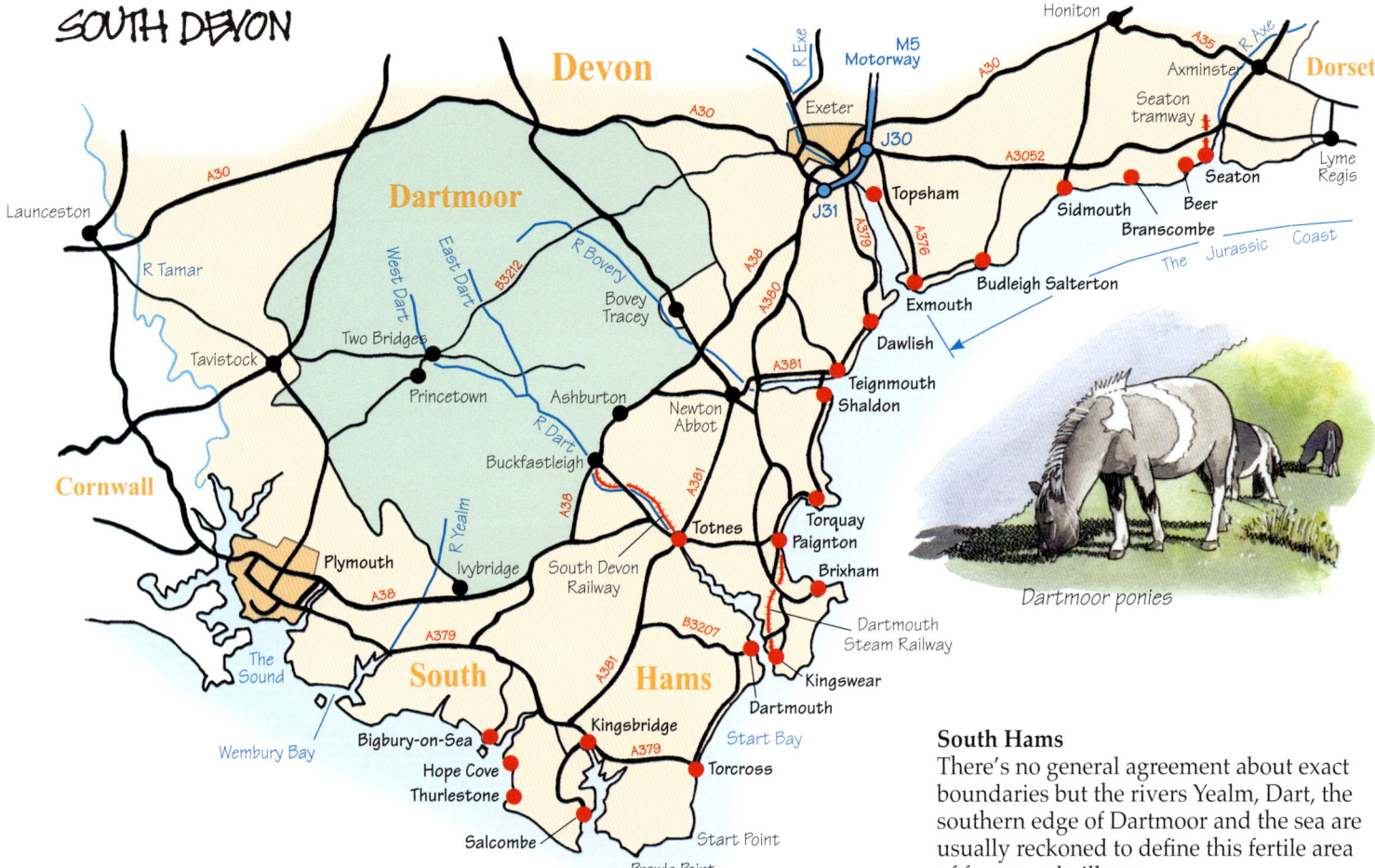

Dartmoor ponies

South Hams
There's no general agreement about exact boundaries but the rivers Yealm, Dart, the southern edge of Dartmoor and the sea are usually reckoned to define this fertile area of farms and villages.

Many of England's favourite holiday resorts are strung along the south Devon coastline like jewels on an antique necklace. Most developed with the arrival of the railway in the 1840s and the popularity of the area with royalty and the aristocracy of the time. They built fashionable villas and mansions overlooking the sea and demanded all the facilities they enjoyed back home in the cities.

Fortunately, much of the elegant Regency and Edwardian architecture survives, despite the coastline being heavily bombed during World War Two. Many of the resorts, particularly those between Sidmouth and Torquay, retain a now slightly old-fashioned charm. Some, such as Exmouth and Teignmouth, have also acquired a modern sophistication as an added attraction.

South of ever-popular but often over-busy Tor Bay, the rural peace of the South Hams is almost like entering a different county, while the great maritime centres of Dartmouth and Salcombe, awash with money and vitality, are always good for life-enhancing visits.

Taking a boat up the River Dart is the perfect river trip and Dartmoor remains the wild and untamed wonder it has always been, with the bonus of some discrete modern management ensuring that it remains so.

Though there was no space in this book to do justice to Exeter, it's an attractive and fascinating city to visit. Plymouth also shouldn't be missed, especially the Barbican area with it's nationally significant maritime history.

Budleigh Salterton

SEATON

One of a series of sedate holiday destinations along this part of the coast, Seaton's elevation to stylish resort began when the railway arrived in the 1860s. Some Victorian and Edwardian architecture survives around the pedestrianised shopping area.

The western end of the town has a quiet and unassuming air, but it's livelier at the other where there's cafés, facilities and a small marina where the River Axe reaches the sea.

With the white cliffs of Beer Head to the east and the red sandstone of Haven Cliff to the west, Seaton is beautifully situated on Lyme Bay. A seawall protects properties along the Esplanade but unfortunately it also cuts off the town from the gently sloping pebble beach.

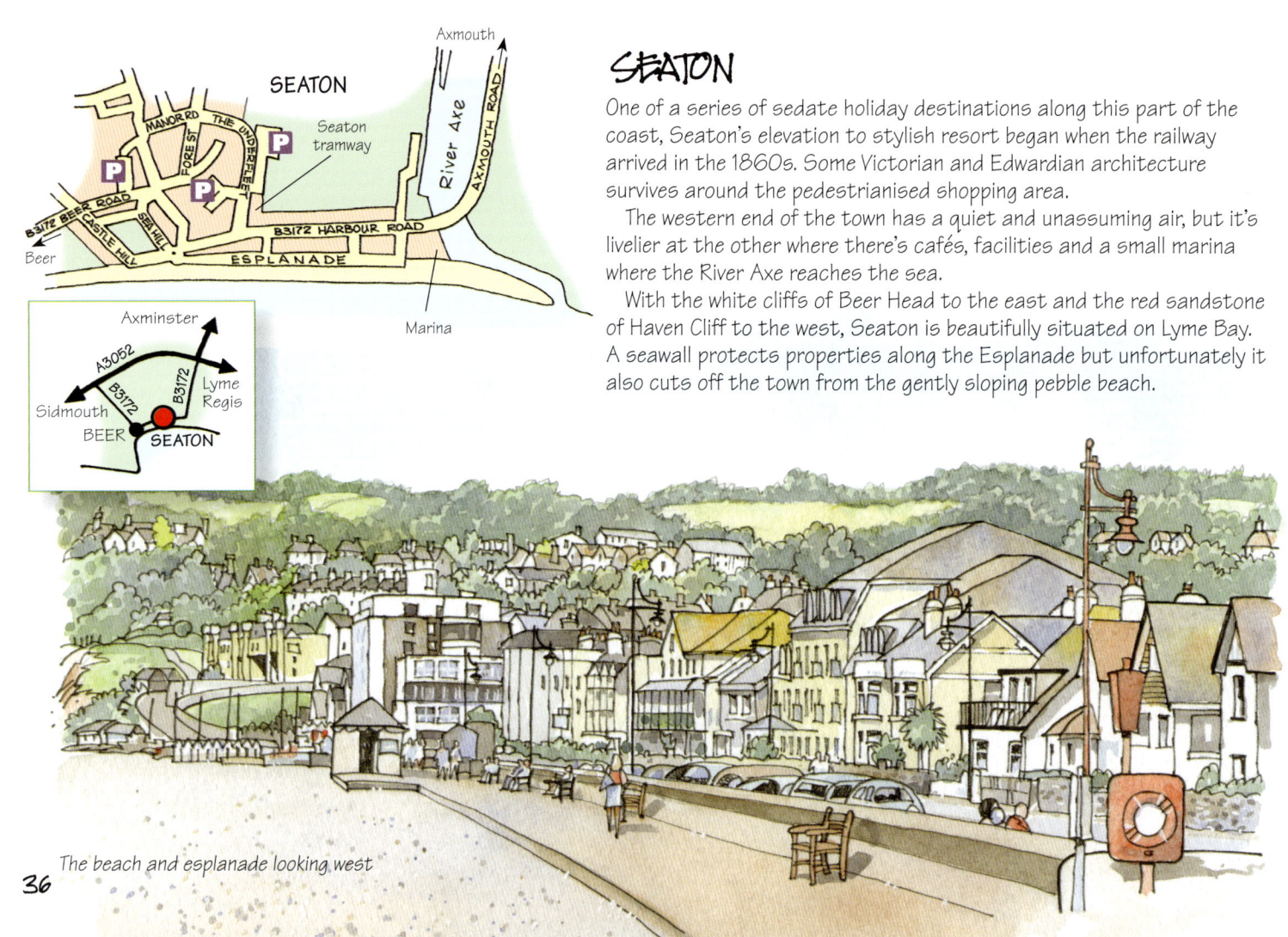

The beach and esplanade looking west

Usage of the train line declined in the 1960s and it was finally closed in 1966. Between 1969 and 1971 tram enthusiast Claude Lane turned the disused rail track into a narrow gauge tramway running three miles along the Axe valley to Colyton. The thirteen heritage tram cars are half scale replicas of classic cars from various cities. One dates back to 1904. The tramway carries around 100,000 passengers a year, many of them wildlife lovers going to enjoy the nature reserves of Seaton Marshes and Colyford Common along the river.

Seaton is a gateway town to the Jurassic Coast, a UNESCO World Heritage Site. For more than six miles from here to Lyme Regis the coast is a torturous series of unstable cliffs tangled with trees and scrub. A haven for wildlife and regarded by naturalists as the last and largest wilderness on the south coast, it can only be reached along the South Devon Coast Path, a section of the route not to be undertaken lightly.

A boat drawn up on the pebble beach

The Axe outlet from Axmouth Road bridge

The tramway terminus off Harbour Road

BEER

The name has nothing to do with the drink; it's a corruption of the old English word *bearu* meaning small wood. The seaside village is not particularly wooded these days but it does enjoy an attractive location snuggled down in a depression in the white cliffs around Lyme Bay with its main street running straight down to a wide pebble beach.

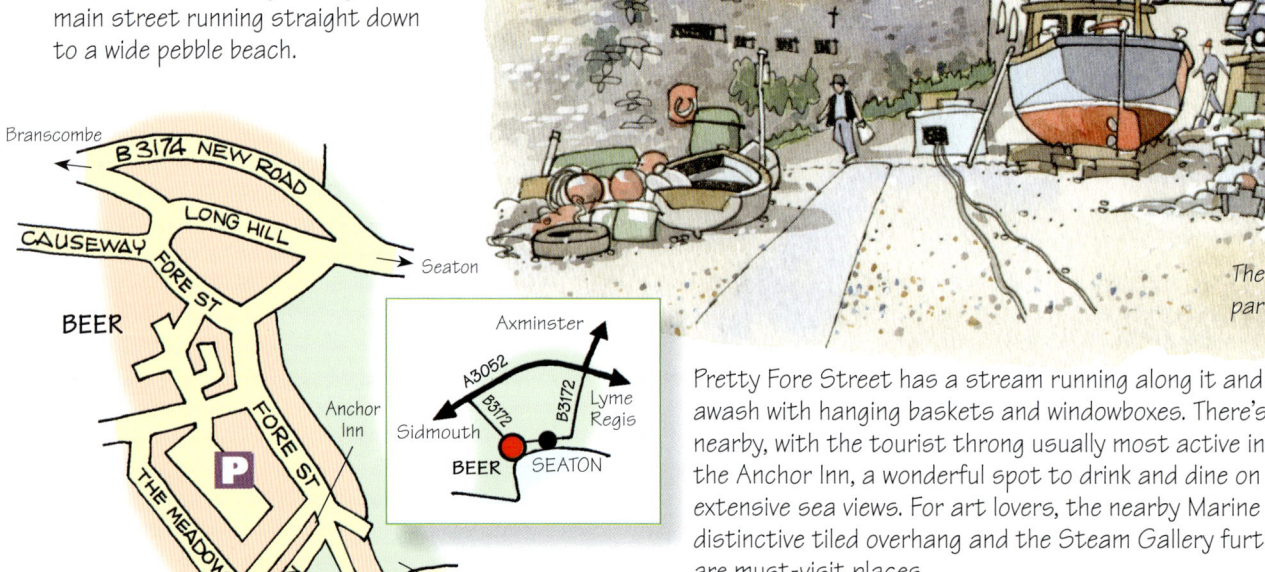

The fisherman's part of the beach

Pretty Fore Street has a stream running along it and in summer is awash with hanging baskets and windowboxes. There's a large car park nearby, with the tourist throng usually most active in the area around the Anchor Inn, a wonderful spot to drink and dine on the clifftop with extensive sea views. For art lovers, the nearby Marine House with its distinctive tiled overhang and the Steam Gallery further up Fore Street are must-visit places.

Set above the working part of the beach, Jubilee Gardens is a great place to sit and admire the fabulous setting of this delightful village.

Common Lane

Beer grew around a smuggler's cove and the caves used to store contraband. Many of the village buildings are faced with flint, a hard glassy stone found in the local chalk rock, such as the remarkable terrace in Common Lane running uphill from the Anchor Inn.

The pebble beach is difficult to walk on so long rubber mats – actually recycled conveyor belts – are laid across it to assist walkers.

Beer beach

Gaily-painted fishing boats on the beach

Beer was once renowned for its lace-making industry, established by Dutch refugees, but these days tourism has largely taken over, though a small fishing fleet still operates from the beach.

Beer quarry caves near the village is a underground limestone complex resulting from 2,000 years of quarrying beer stone, a creamy-grey fine textured stone that is relatively soft when first mined but hardens with exposure to air to become as hard as Portland stone. Quarrying ceased in the early 20th century but the stone was used in many fine buildings, including St Paul's Cathedral, Westminster Abbey and Windsor Castle.

BRANSCOMBE

One of the prettiest villages in south Devon – and possibly also the longest – Branscombe straggles for around a mile along narrow roads down steep-sided combes, terminating at a pebble beach, Branscombe Mouth, part of the East Devon & Dorset Jurassic Coast.

Branscombe is picture perfect with thatched cottages, a couple of 14th-century inns and an ancient church, St Winifred's which dates back to the Norman Conquest. There's even a thatched blacksmith's shop, a watermill – and a brewery! How perfect is that?

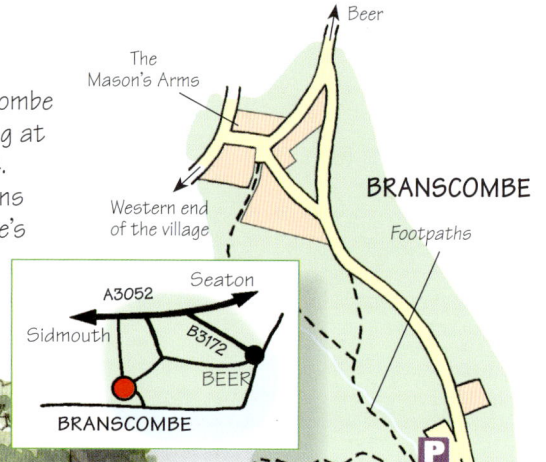

The Mason's Arms at the seaward end of the village

Branscombe was thrust into the national limelight in January 2007 when the 62,000 tonne container ship MSC Napoli ran aground offshore and scavengers from all over the country descended to pillage its cargo. The only sign of it today is the ship's enormous anchor displayed on a plinth by the seafront.

The Mason's Arms – its name a reminder of the stone quarrying in nearby Beer Stone Caves – has been a hostelry since 1360, with ship's beams, slate floors and open fires inside and tables outside. The Fountain Head, at the less visited end of the village, exudes similar good cheer and character with a speciality range of local brews always on tap.

Branscombe is a popular starting point for walks, especially along the Coast Path. The Hooken Landslip occurred in 1790 when part of the cliff near the village collapsed leaving great turrets of white stone, the Branscombe Pinnacles.

Around two miles long, the gently sloping, south-facing pebble beach is one of the least spoilt in south Devon. A few fishing boats pull up on it and some can be hired for mackerel fishing trips or scenic coastal excursions.

The thatched Sea Shanty restaurant and tea room has a small shop and a large car park – once a coal yard.

Former coastguard cottages

Branscombe thatched cottages

The Sea Shanty

Branscombe Mouth

SIDMOUTH

The grand aristocrat of the East Devon coast with nearly 500 listed buildings, Sidmouth sits regally in the valley of the River Sid between the steep red sandstone cliffs of Salcombe Hill and Peak Hill. With a mile-long esplanade alongside a broad pebble beach, Regency architecture, elegant bow-fronted houses, wrought-iron balconies and white-painted façades, it's no wonder that John Betjeman described Sidmouth as 'a town caught still in a timeless charm'. A sentiment that's largely true today. Many of the independent shops along the narrow pedestrianised streets have kept their original 19th-century fronts.

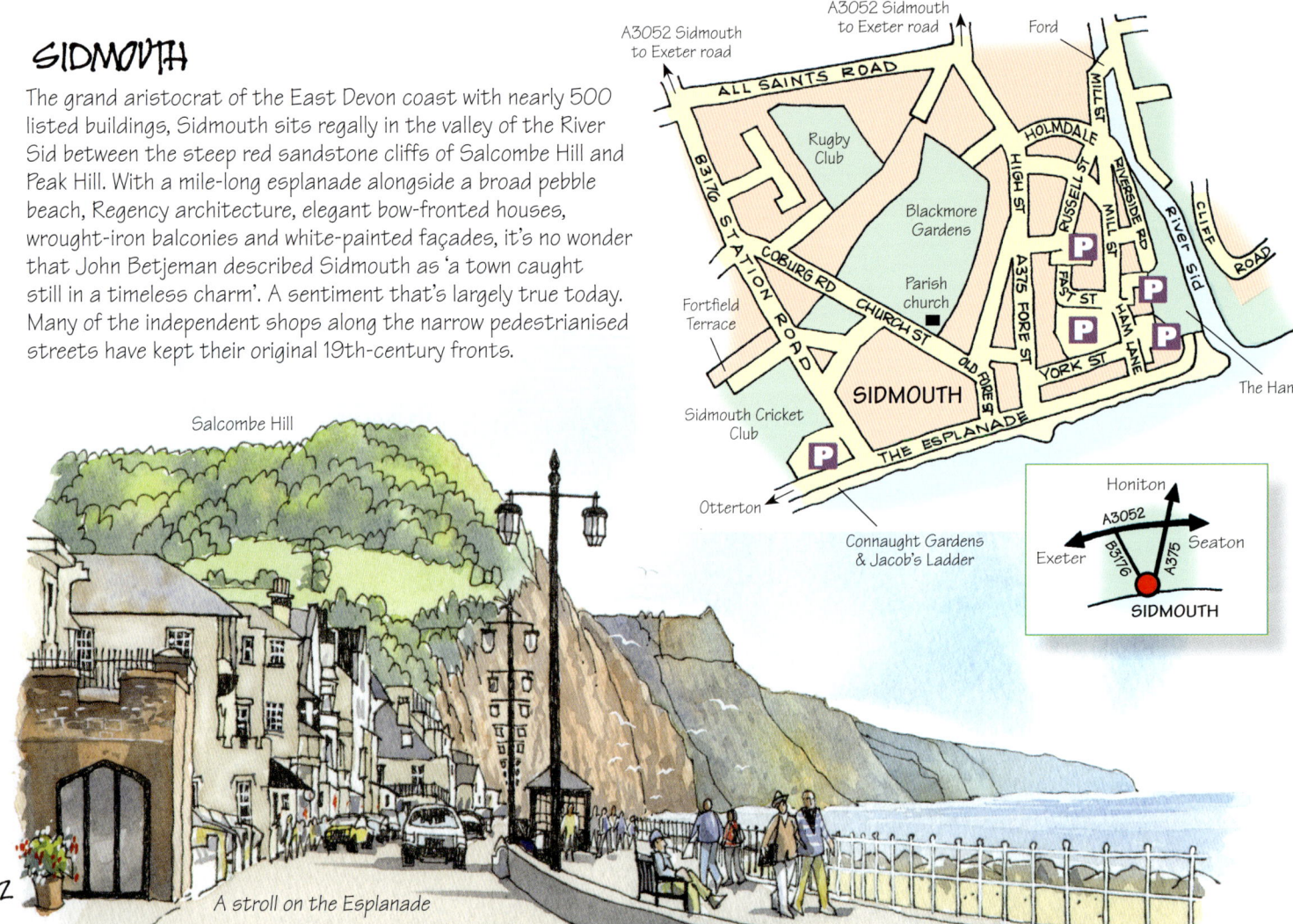

A stroll on the Esplanade

Jacob's Ladder

Sidmouth enjoyed royal patronage during the early 19th century, among them Grand Duchess Hélène of Russia, sister-in-law to the tsar, who lived at Fortfield Terrace, a Regency masterpiece of white façade and canopied balconies which still looks across an immaculate croquet and cricket ground.

Less elegant, but nevertheless popular with tourists, is Jacob's Ladder, a simple series of wooden steps linking Connaught Gardens with the beach below.

Motorists who enjoy childish pleasures (me, me, me!) can splash their way through an impressive ford where the River Sid crosses the road at the end of Mill Street.

Ladram Bay
Peak Hill
Connaught Gardens & Jacob's Ladder
The Esplanade
Sidmouth's wonderful setting

Fortfield Terrace

43

BUDLEIGH SALTERTON

Quieter than neighbouring Sidmouth, Budleigh Salterton became a popular resort in the wake of its grander neighbour.

Situated on the west side of the Otter estuary the town was originally called Ottermouth. The 'Salterton' part of the name came from the salt-panning carried out by monks evaporating sea water during the 13th century.

Budleigh's a rather old-fashioned place that suits the elderly folk who have retired here, drawn by the quieter pace of life and the respectability and charm that once attracted such figures as Noël Coward and P.G. Woodhouse.

The town has few chain stores. Shops are generally proudly independent with old-world service and courtesy.

The western end of the beach

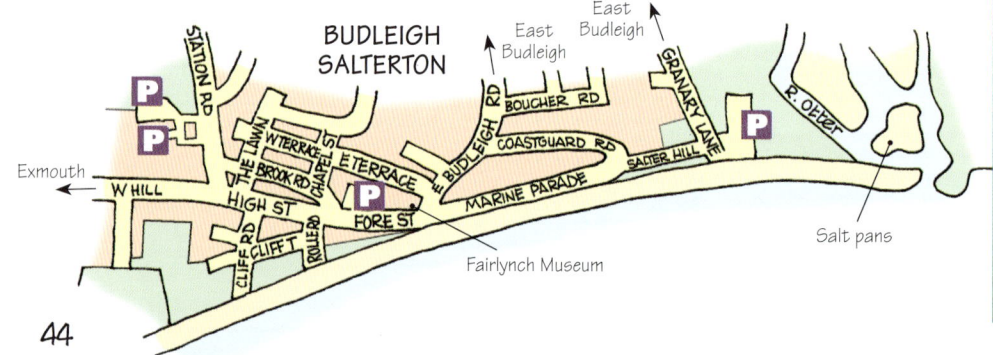

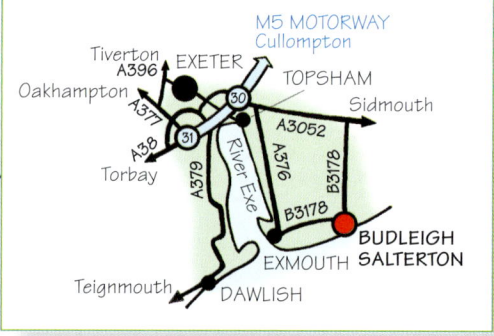

Fairlynch Museum

A 19th-century ornamental rustic cottage or *cottage orné* in Fore Street, one of several in the area, houses the Fairlynch Museum & Arts Centre that celebrates the area's history and geology.

The town's beach consists of large, rounded pebbles, fallout from the crumbly, red sandstone cliffs. Beach huts are a popular feature of the south Devon seaside and Budleigh has some top of the range examples. The one illustrated here sold for £200 in 2011 – but that didn't include the site!

Sold!

In keeping with the town's gentility, the River Otter enters the sea quietly – almost a trickle. It was not always so. In the Middle Ages ships sailed up the river as far as Otterton but a pebble bridge gradually formed across the mouth and the river eventually silted up, ending the sea-going trade.

The ancient salt pans by the river mouth now provide a rich habitat for wildlife. Redshank, greenshank, plovers and other migrant birds are regular visitors.

Budleigh beach huts

The western end of the beach

EXMOUTH

Set serenely at the mouth of the Exe estuary, Exmouth is a quintessential seaside resort with two miles of golden sands, some graceful examples of Georgian and Victorian architecture, and a proud history as an important port for over 800 years.

The estuary has silted up over the years and the dock area has now been turned into a luxury marina with the accompanying apartments and marine services. Exmouth is renowned for its sailing, windsurfing and kite-surfing, although the strong currents in the estuary are no place for novices, who usually start on the Duck pond at the north side of town.

The sandy beach is the star attraction here, by far the best and biggest in south Devon. All the facilities for a traditional seaside holiday line the winding esplanade, with beach huts, Punch & Judy shows and donkey rides on the beach in summer. There's two large car parks and roadside parking along the whole length of the promenade, but Exmouth is extremely popular, so whenever the sun is out, get there early!

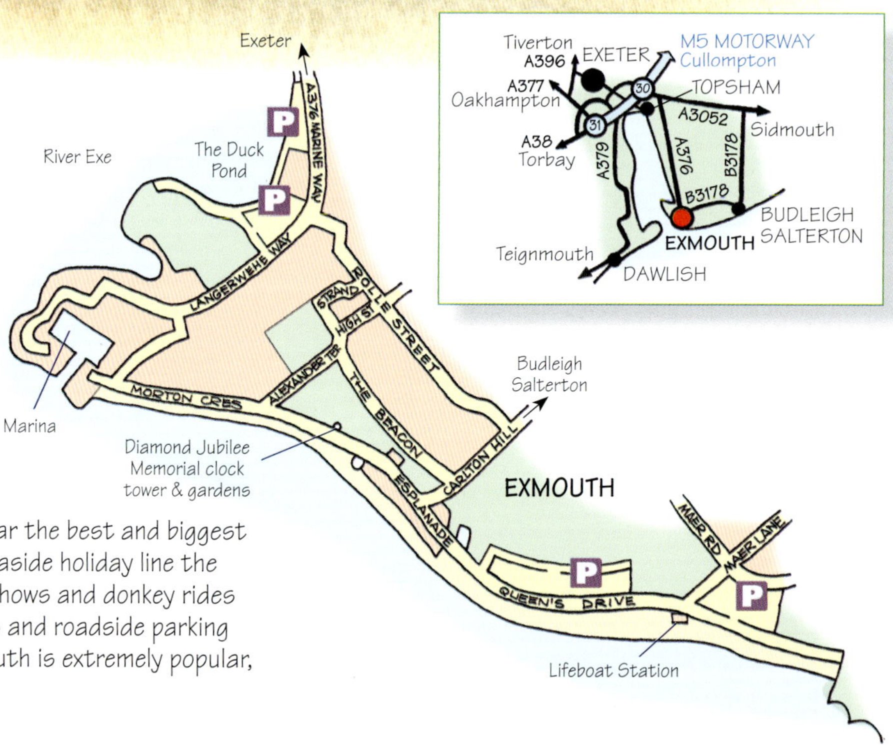

Exmouth's finest architecture is concentrated on a hill known as The Beacon, overlooking the seafront. The wives of Nelson and Byron were amongst the town's fashionable visitors, with Lady Nelson spending her final years at No. 6 The Beacon.

The pedestrianised Magnolia Centre is the town's main shopping area with more individual shops to be found down the side streets. The Café Quarter just off the Strand boasts a wealth of cafés, boutiques and gift shops.

Exmouth has much to offer the discerning visitor, but just to walk along that fabulous beach and enjoy the views out to sea and across the estuary makes a visit worthwhile.

View towards the town from the Esplanade

The western end of the beach

TOPSHAM

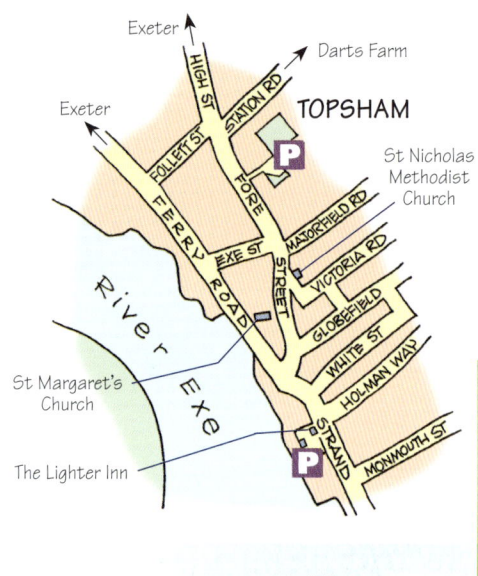

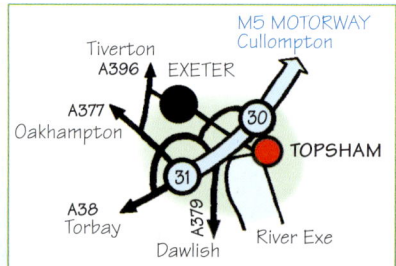

Loved by its locals and savoured by visitors, Topsham is one of south Devon's hidden gems. Now officially part of Exeter, the delightful small town, set on the Exe estuary and tucked up to the busy M5 motorway, miraculously maintains its own distinct identity. There's attractive buildings, river walks, many characterful shops, restaurants, tea shops and inns, and plenty of quiet places to just sit and watch the boats go by.

The Exe estuary is the largest in Devon and its many sandbanks and mudflats teem with small creatures which attract huge flocks of resident and migratory birds. The geese at the Ferry Road slip are scaringly friendly!

Parking in Topsham can be difficult. Of two central car parks the largest one at the Lighter Inn is the best bet. You might be lucky to find a roadside space in the High Street or you can try the rugby ground on the northern outskirts of the village.

The classic view of Topsham from St Margaret's churchyard

St Nicholas Methodist Church

A Fore Street gallery

Cheese shop in Fore Street

An important port since roman times, Topsham prospered hugely from the European (and later the transatlantic) wool trade after a weir was built just upriver, effectively cutting off Exeter from sea-going ships. When that business faltered at the end of the 18th century, shipbuilding and its subsidiary activities, such as chain-making and rope-making became Topsham's main industries until well into the 19th century.

These days the estuary is almost totally given over to leisure activities, but boat maintenance and restoration continues at the riverside jetties.

Many of Topsham's handsome buildings date from the town's heyday, the trade with Holland being celebrated in the characteristic Dutch-style houses in the Strand, some built from bricks imported as ballast from Holland.

Ferry Road and Fore Street converge at the oldest part of the quay, where the Lighter Inn now occupies the old Custom House, said to date from the early 14th century. A former warehouse nearby is packed to the gunnels with antiques.

Modern chainstores are conspicuously absent from Topsham's narrow streets. The independent shops are generally aimed at the comfortably well-off local and visitor clientele.

A mile out of town, Dart's Farm has taken the farm shop concept and turned it into virtually a complete shopping village, with a variety of outlets selling everything from organic food to binoculars for bird-watchers.

Dutch-influenced house

The junction of Ferry Road & Fore Street

DAWLISH

Another of the sedate seaside resorts favoured by 19th-century holidaymakers, Dawlish has some fine Georgian and Victorian architecture but lacks the grandeur of the flashier places. But in a good way – it's all part of the town's old-fashioned charm.

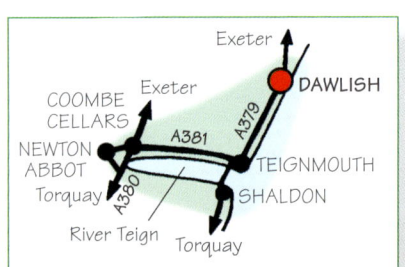

The view west from the rail station footbridge

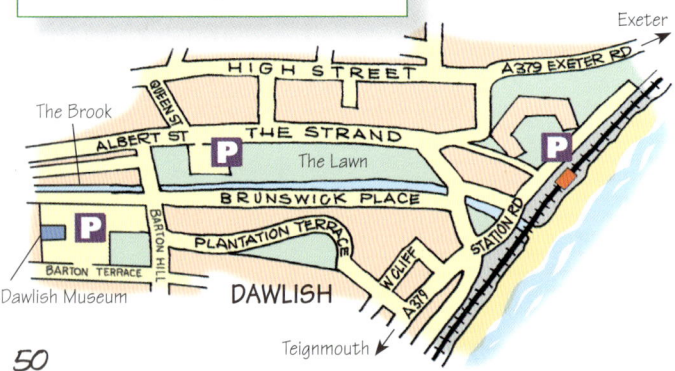

Once a small fishing village, Dawlish blossomed when the railway arrived in 1846 and tourism became the main industry. Jane Austin and Charles Dickens were literary visitors and made reference to the town in their books. Isambard Kingdom Brunel built the station and a railway line along the sea wall, a considerable engineering achievement and a huge scenic attraction for Victorian travellers. The exciting train ride remains and a tunnel gives access to the beach but the railway sadly cuts off the sea from the town. Over a mile long, the beach is a mixture of sand and red shingle. At each end, craggy red cliffs rise steeply from the sea, presenting a constant hazard to the railway as chunks can break off during violent storms.

The south side of The Lawn

The rail station

The Lawn slices through the centre of the town. Once swampy marshland, it was reclaimed in 1808 and transformed into an ornamental park with trim flower beds, meandering paths, torbay palms and, at the western end, a pristine bowling green.

Fine houses and shops line The Strand and Brunswick Place, the two streets along the edges of The Lawn. Away from the seafront, Dawlish is a maze of narrow streets and alleys, with tiny, cobbled Albert Street worth exploring.

The famous black swans of Dawlish, natives of Australia, were introduced to the town in the early 20th-century by Dawlish-born John Nash. Later in life he emigrated to New Zealand but made frequent visits back to his birthplace. The black swan has been the town emblem for over forty years.

There are now over a dozen swans that cruise up and down The Brook flowing through the Lawn. Another 50 or so ornamental wildfowl are kept in an enclosure on the riverbank.

The north side of The Lawn

TEIGNMOUTH

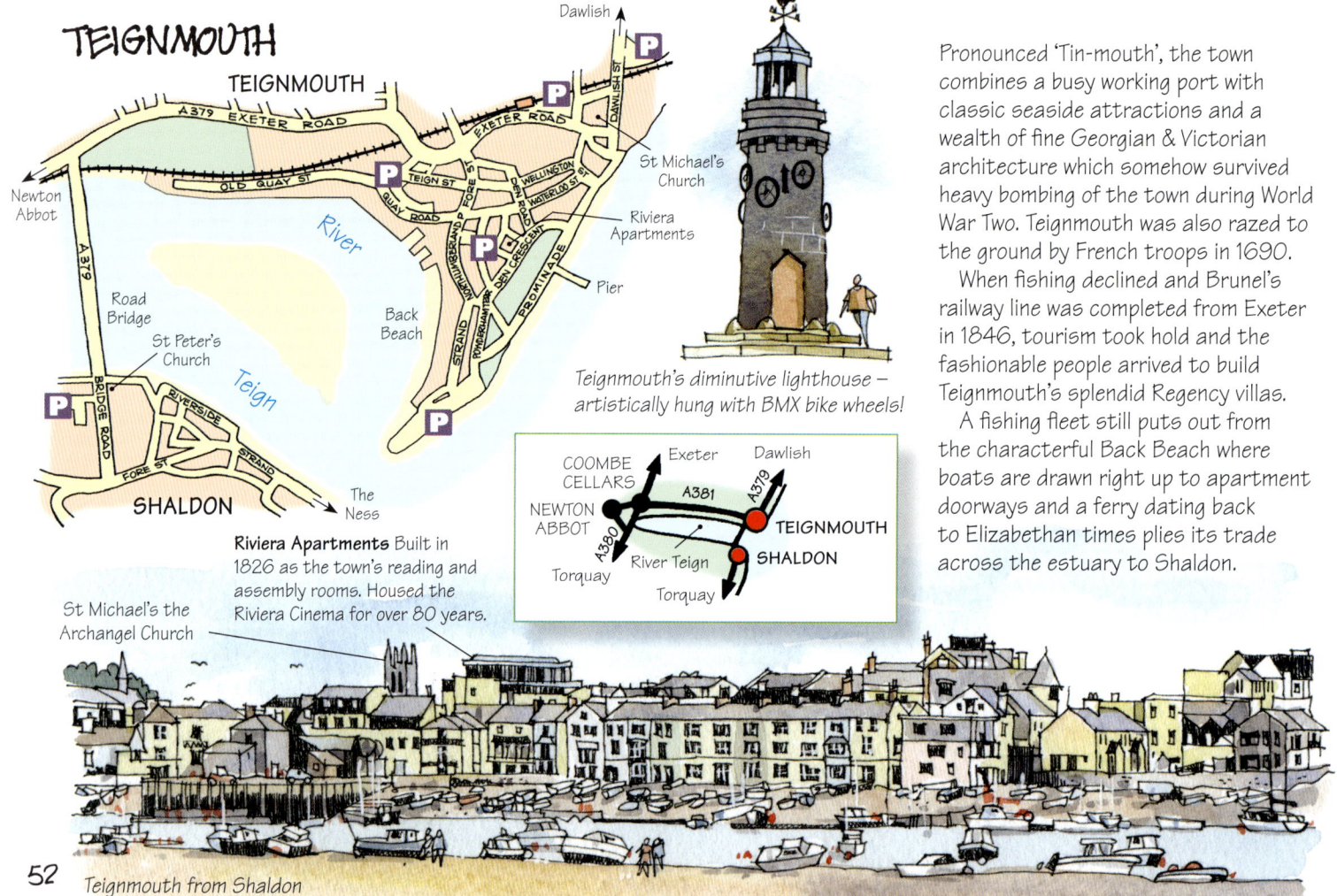

Teignmouth's diminutive lighthouse – artistically hung with BMX bike wheels!

Riviera Apartments Built in 1826 as the town's reading and assembly rooms. Housed the Riviera Cinema for over 80 years.

Teignmouth from Shaldon

Pronounced 'Tin-mouth', the town combines a busy working port with classic seaside attractions and a wealth of fine Georgian & Victorian architecture which somehow survived heavy bombing of the town during World War Two. Teignmouth was also razed to the ground by French troops in 1690.

When fishing declined and Brunel's railway line was completed from Exeter in 1846, tourism took hold and the fashionable people arrived to build Teignmouth's splendid Regency villas.

A fishing fleet still puts out from the characterful Back Beach where boats are drawn right up to apartment doorways and a ferry dating back to Elizabethan times plies its trade across the estuary to Shaldon.

Dawlish Exmouth

Teignmouth, as seen from the Ness at Shaldon

The Triangle

The Den is the centre of holiday activities with play and sports areas; lawns and flowerbeds; a long sandy beach almost as red as the surrounding cliffs; and the wonderful old-style pier.

The Triangle, a pedestrianised central square, forms the hub of café society, with a maze of narrow alleys and old maritime inns of the old town a delight to explore.

The bridge across the Teign to Shaldon saves a detour around Newton Abbot of some fourteen miles, so has been an integral part of local life since the first wooden crossing was built in 1827. Tolls were abandoned in 1948 and strengthening of the present rather switchback construction was completed in 2002.

The Pier Built in the 1860s and once marked the segregation point between male and female bathers

The Ness

The Promenade

The village green and war memorial

St Peter's Church

The Ferry Boat Inn

SHALDON

The village of Shaldon has an air of unspoiled period charm that's often bypassed by the seasonal crowds streaming across the Teign Bridge for the more lively delights of Teignmouth. The Strand runs along the edge of the estuary where small boats of interesting vintages litter the red shingle beach. Characterful pubs and bistros with chalkboards of fishing specials jostle for space amongst flower-decked Georgian houses, packed closely together. There's a great view of Teignmouth's long Back Beach across the estuary, especially when enjoyed while taking refreshment in the Ferry Boat Inn garden.

In contrast to the rest of the cheery village, the magnificent edifice of St Peter's Church lurks gloomily beside the road bridge. Completed in 1902, it's a fabulous monument to the Victorian 'hell and damnation' brand of religion. The interior is just as cheerless, but beautifully kept and oddly uplifting.

A great tree-topped cliff known as The Ness rises dramatically from the seashore with a remarkable tunnel through the rock giving access to Ness Cove, a tiny beach on the other side of the headland. There's a car park on The Ness, just off the Torquay Road as it climbs out of the village.

The Ness

Shaldon

TORQUAY

Set regally at the northern end of the great sweep of Tor Bay and scattered across seven pine-covered hills plunging to an azure-coloured sea, Torquay has a a lot of natural attributes going for it.

With the arrival of the railway in the 1840s, the sleepy fishing village with an equable climate grew into a sophisticated resort attracting the high echelons of Victorian society, who built grand Italianate villas on the hillsides.

The Pavilion

The Harbour

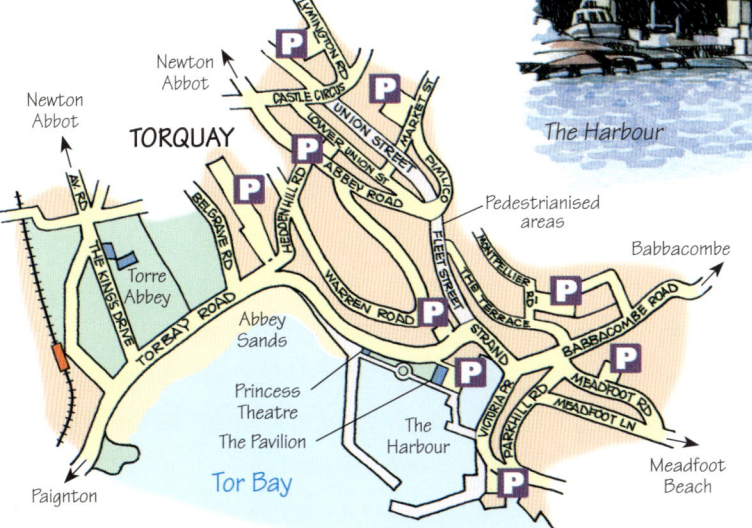

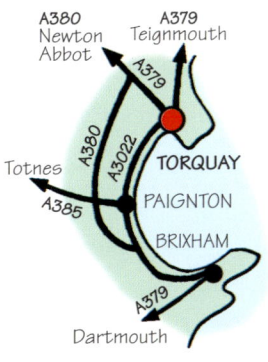

Born in Torquay, Agatha Christie spent much of her life in the town, roller-skating on Princess Pier and honeymooning at the Grand Hotel. She would have known the copper-domed Edwardian Pavilion, opened in 1912 and adorned with cherubs and flowery scrolls. Once an elegant ballroom, it now houses an eclectic collection of independent shops.

Tor Bay from Royal Terrace Gardens

The main town beach, Abbey Sands, along Torbay Road, is narrow and quickly fills up when the sun comes out. There are larger beaches at Babbacombe and Oddicombe.

A huge amount of money has been spent on developing the harbour area. The steps of Royal Terrace Gardens wind up the cliff above Princess Pier and the theatre, giving sensational views across the bay, especially at night. With berths for over 400 craft, and cafés and shops lining the quayside, the marina is an attractive area to wander round. Harbour Bridge crosses to Beacon Quay, where LED lights on a 23ft (7m) painted steel ring spell out 'vanishing point' in morse code as a memorial to the troops that set off from here on D-Day and never returned.

Restaurants and cafés along the Strand are at the heart of Torquay, with the main pedestrianised shopping areas of Fleet Street and Union Street leading off.

Torquay's long-established attractions are always worth a visit: the Model Village at Babbacombe; Kent's Cavern; Torre Abbey and Gardens. Sadly though, and despite the still wealthy areas and millionaire's power boats docked in the marina, the glamour of the town has faded. Many of the fine buildings have been turned into bars or clubs and Torquay has become one of south Devon's premier party destinations. Some of us may not like it, but it's often the big-spending party-goers who keep fragile seaside economies ticking over.

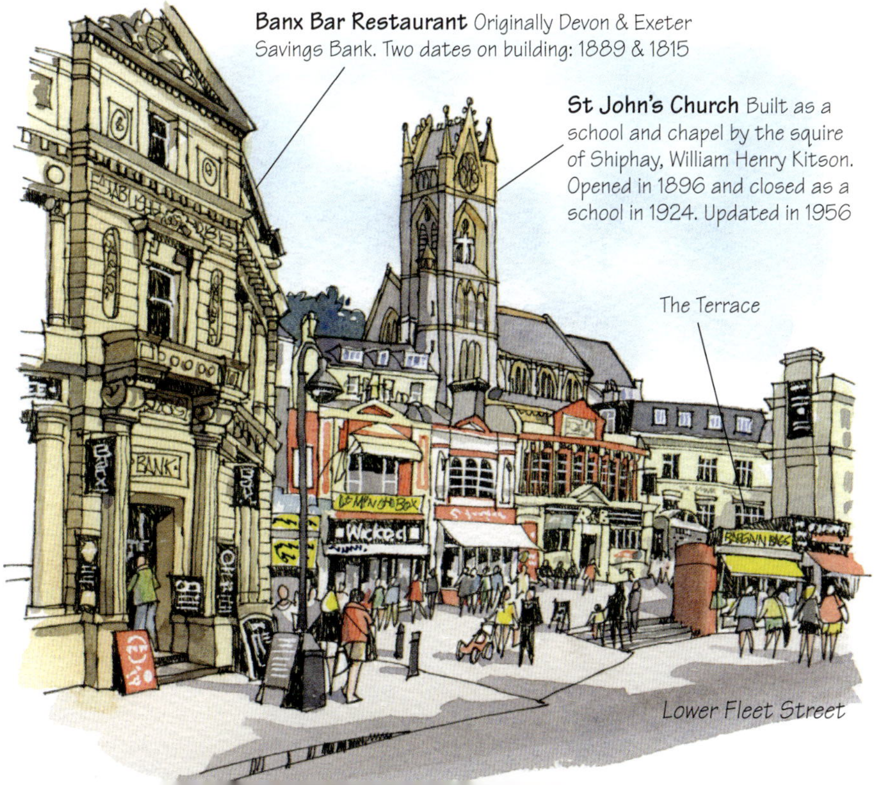

Banx Bar Restaurant Originally Devon & Exeter Savings Bank. Two dates on building: 1889 & 1815

St John's Church Built as a school and chapel by the squire of Shiphay, William Henry Kitson. Opened in 1896 and closed as a school in 1924. Updated in 1956

The Terrace

Lower Fleet Street

The classic scene

COCKINGTON

Only a mile or so from central Torquay, there's a totally different environment. Tagged by its detractors as just a chocolate-box stage set, Cockington Village nestles deeply in a hidden valley, a haven of rural peace. The famous view of thatched cottages and smithy, seen in countless photos, is indeed a twee classic, but away from the carefully preserved artifice the remainder of the 420 acres of parkland is a wonderful setting for a leisurely stroll.

The landscaped grounds of Cockington Court include an unusual cricket pitch set in a grassy bowl, working craft studios behind the big house, rose gardens and a handsome 13th-century church, all set in a colourful arboretum of trees.

A terraced tea room provides refreshment or try the thatched Drum Inn, designed by Edwin Lutyens in 1934, the most 'modern' building in the village.

Looking north, along the beach

PAIGNTON

The central one of the trio of 'English Riviera' resorts and often regarded as a poor relation to Torquay, Paignton has a cheerful and carefree air about it that's sadly lacking in its more pretentious neighbour. The town is an unabashed traditional English seaside holiday destination with a few added modern thrills and spills.

Paignton faces east, out to sea, sheltered on the leeward side by rolling Devon countryside with its fiery-red soil. Its greatest asset over Torquay are the two long, ruddy-red beaches, gently sloping for safe family bathing. Lawns and gardens back the promenade and there's a pretty harbour, built in 1838, at the southern end.

The Victorian pier at the centre point was put up for sale in 2013 with an asking price of nearly £2 million. Designed by architect George Soudon Bridgeman, the original 780ft (238m) long pier opened in 1879 and was rebuilt after being destroyed by fire in 1919. The modern pier is awash with all the gaudy glories of the traditional English seaside – slot machines, kiss-me-quick hats, candy floss and much, much more!

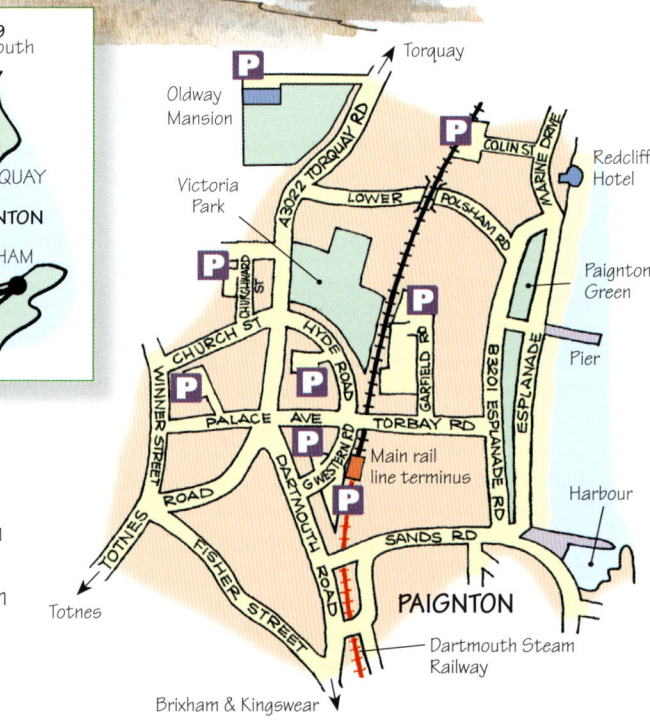

A typical beach shop on the pier approach

Contrasting architecture at the end of the Esplanade

Paignton Zoo, set in 75 acres a mile out of town on the Totnes Road, is one of the largest in the country, with the animals shown in natural-looking habitats.

Oldway Mansion lies just off the Torquay Road, surrounded by lush parkland. Originally built in 1902 by the US sewing-machine tycoon, Isaac Merritt Singer, it was extensively rebuilt by his son, Paris, as a gaudy, neoclassical extravaganza. Paris lived here with the dancer Isadora Duncan, who was famously strangled when her scarf tangled in the wheel of her car. The 1969 biopic film *Isadora*, starring Vanessa Redgrave, was filmed here.

The Dartmouth Steam Railway runs a regular service along a scenic six-mile route between Paignton and Kinsgwear. The line, completed in 1864, was due for closure in 1968 but was eventually sold to the Dart Valley Railway Company in 1972. Unusual amongst heritage railways, it's a commercial operation, so doesn't rely on volunteers or charitable donations.

Terrace of apartments and B&Bs on Esplanade Road

BRIXHAM

The third of the Torbay trio of tourist destinations, Brixham has a more rough and ready feel about it, less touristy, as befits its status as a swashbuckling fishing port with a seafaring history stretching back over 900 years. Fishing is still a buoyant industry here with a multi-million development of the quayside fish market recently completed and over a hundred boats kept busy.

Beneath the steep hillsides crowded with terraces of colour-washed houses, the lively harbour always has a cheerful look even on the greyest of days, while along the Quay, the Strand and King Street, gift shops, cafes and seafood restaurants jostle for tourist trade.

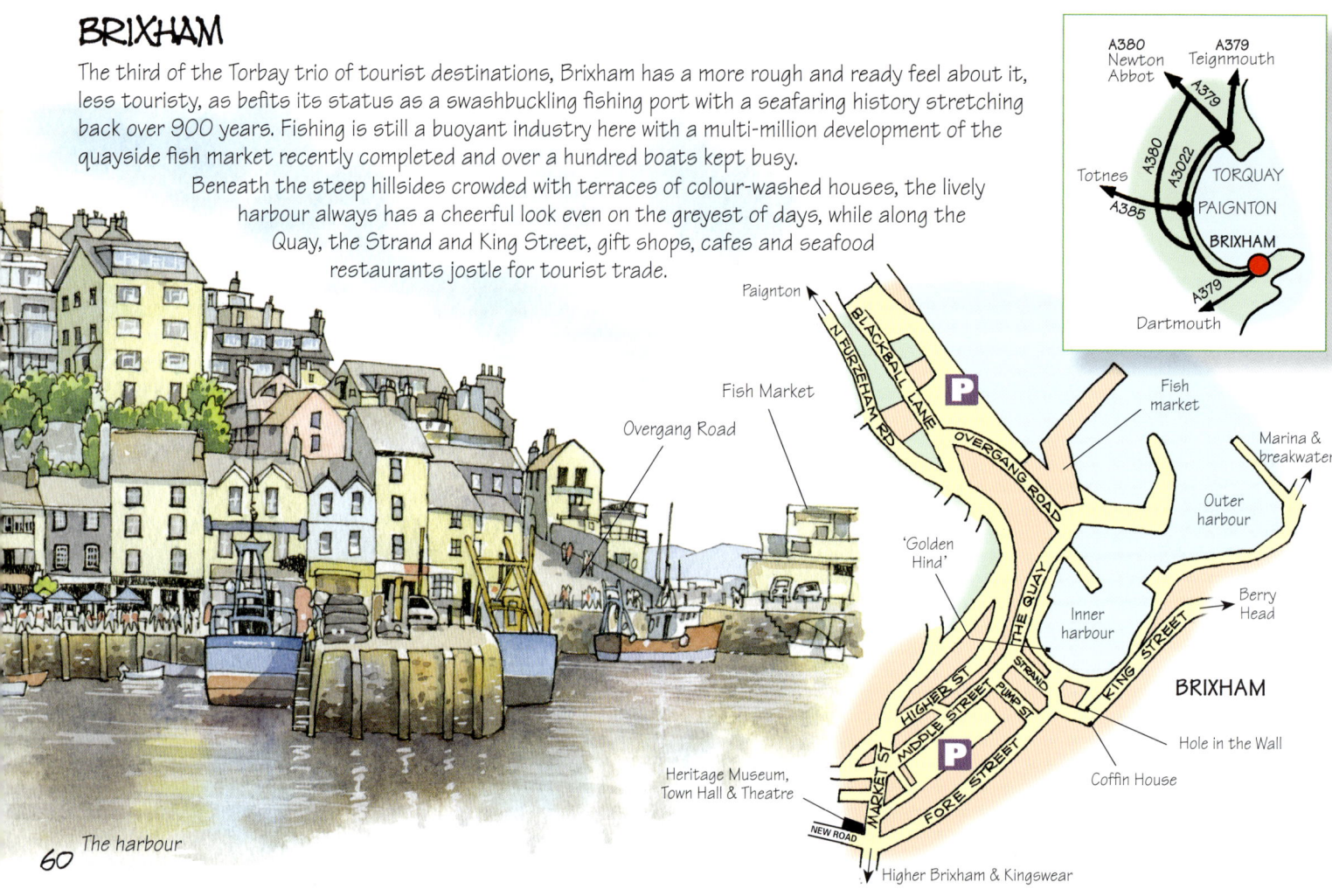

The harbour

The end of the long breakwater

A walkway on the King Street side of the harbour passes an impressive marina and ends at a small, pebbly beach. For a really bracing walk continue along the mile-long breakwater that provides fine views of the town and across the bay to Torquay.

A full-sized replica of Sir Francis Drake's Golden Hind, which circumnavigated the globe in 1577, has been moored in the inner harbour since 1963. The onboard museum offers a sanitised glimpse into the world of the 16th-century sailor, but the asking price of £360,000 for the replica's sale in 2013 placed it squarely in the 21st-century market place.

Oddly, the original ship and Drake had little connection with Brixham. William of Orange, later William the third of of 'Great Britain & Ireland', whose statue stands on the quayside, had even less, apart from landing in Brixham with his Dutch army in 1688 proclaiming that 'the protestant religion I will maintain'.

The Golden Hind replica

The Coffin House

The 17th-century Coffin House at the bottom of King Street is another of Brixham's oddities, bolstered by the tale of a father who was asked for the hand in marriage of his daughter but said he would rather 'see her in a coffin, before she wed'. So the future son-in-law bought the Coffin House and returned to the father, saying, 'Your wishes are met'. Amused by this, the father gave his blessing.

Across the road from The Coffin House, the tiny Hole in the Wall pub gamely lives up to its name. This part of King Street could easily be called 'Curio Corner'.

Brixham Heritage Museum has been housed in the former police station on New Road since 1976 with a Maritime Gallery added in 1990. It's packed with everything you ever wanted to know about Brixham – and more!

Brixham Theatre, next door, shows films and stages several live shows a year, performed by local groups.

The town hall and market hall was built, along with the theatre, in 1886. The building occupies the site of the former Naval Reservoir, from where pipes were laid to the harbour to supply water for naval ships.

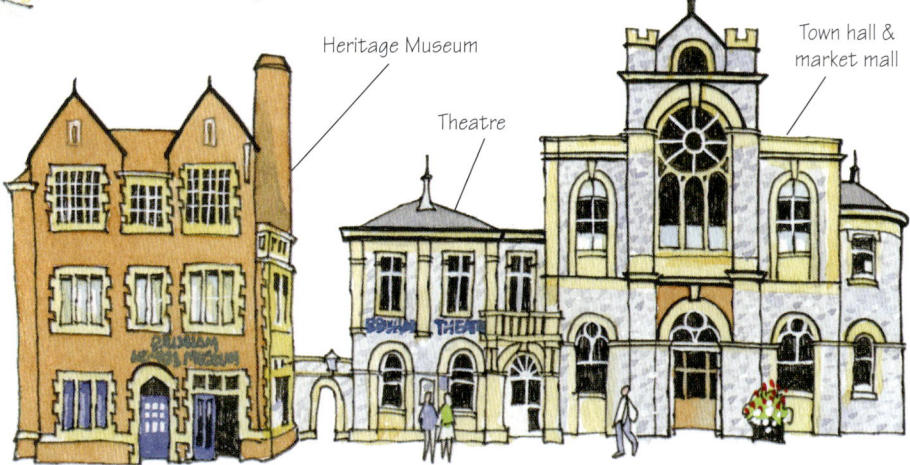

Buildings on the corner of New Road and Market Street

BERRY HEAD

A terrific walk winds through woodland up to Berry Head, one of the area's unsung gems. Whether your interest is rare plants, sea birds, history, technology or just enjoying fantastic views, this is the place for you. You can join the path at the Berry Head Hotel, once the grand home of the vicar of All Saint's Church, Brixham, the Reverend Henry Francis Lyte, who wrote the hymn *Abide With Me* while watching the sunset over Torbay.

The limestone headland, once extensively quarried, is now a nature reserve attracting huge colonies of nesting sea birds. The guillemot colony is one of the largest on the south coast. Berry Head is also a haven for many wild plants, and its caves are home to the endangered greater horseshoe bat.

An Iron Age fort on the headland was destroyed when fortifications, mostly still standing, were built during the Napoleonic Wars to protect the Torbay naval ships against an invasion by the French.

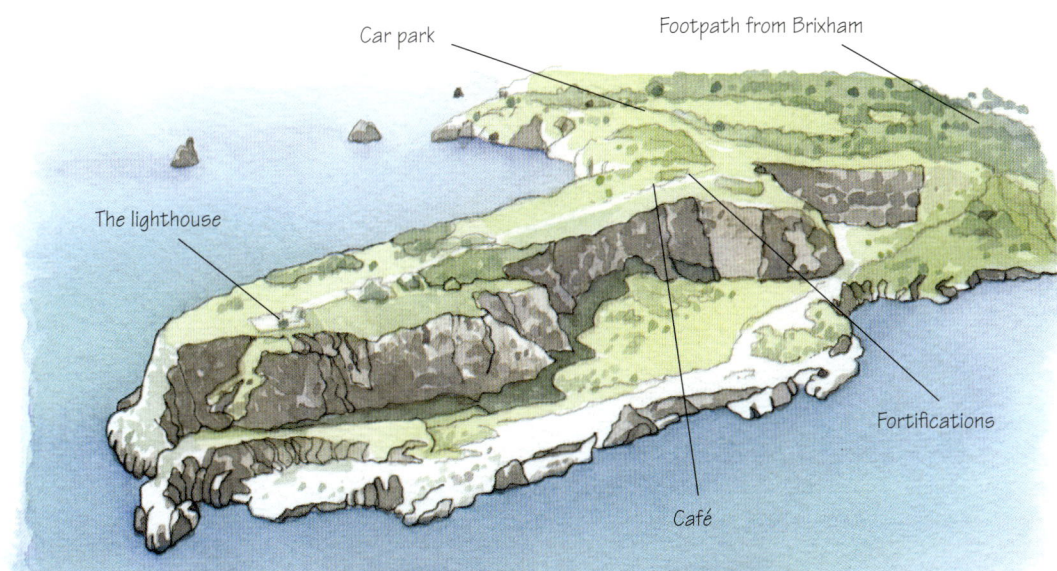

Built in 1906, the lighthouse was converted to run on acetylene in 1921, but since 1994 has been powered by mains electricity. At 191ft (67m) above sea level it's claimed to be the highest lighthouse in Britain. But as the actual building is only a few feet high it can also be called the smallest.

You can also drive to Berry Head from central Brixham, through a holiday camp and along a narrow lane to the car park on the Head. Just follow the signs.

The lighthouse

DARTMOUTH

As the River Dart is about to enter the sea, it deepens, widens and slows, as if in salute to the historic harbour town of Dartmouth, one of the finest deep water anchorages on the South Coast, steeped in a rich maritime history spanning hundreds of years. In an unrivalled setting, tiers of houses clinging to the hillside make the town a dramatic backdrop to all the boating activities offshore.

St Barnabas Church Built 1831. Now the Dartmouth Apprentice restaurant

Bayard's Cove

Dartmouth from Kingswear

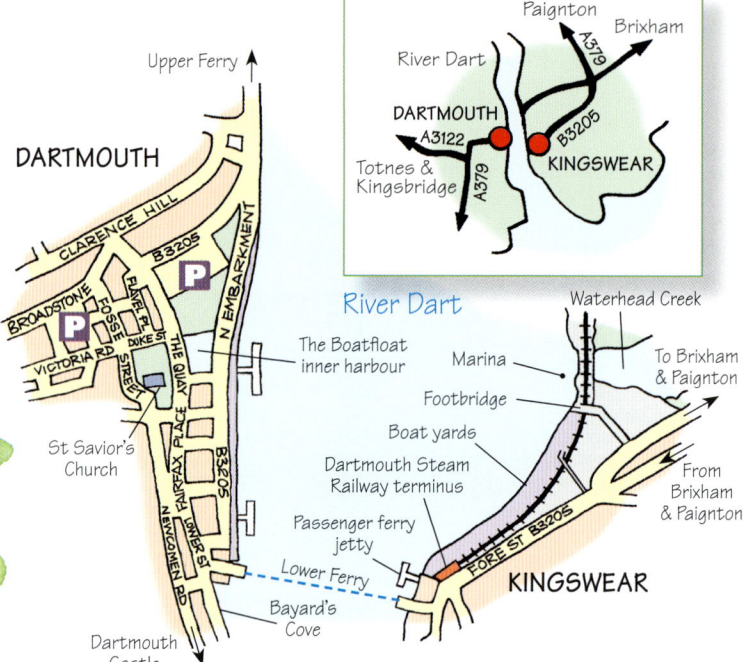

Dartmouth has been an important port since Norman times with the maritime connection continuing today. Fishing and freight are some of the harbour's main activities and, despite a recent threat of closure, officers still train at the imposing Royal Naval College overlooking the town. The huge 138-acre, shore-based college was built in 1905 to replace the floating training base. Since then thousands of British Royal Navy officers have passed out from the college – including four members of the Royal family.

Free of through traffic, Dartmouth is a convivial place to stroll, though you need to be alert to vehicles cruising round looking for somewhere to park. Car parks are not one of Dartmouth's many attributes. The largest, behind the Embankment, soon fills up.

Ancient timber-framed buildings overlook the novel Boatfloat inner harbour, with many more scattered around the narrow streets. The Butterwalk, which now houses the museum, is particularly striking. Fosse Street has interesting small shops, restaurants and galleries. At the top of the street, the 14th-century Church of St Saviour was rebuilt in the 1630s, incorporating timber from the captured flagship of the Spanish Armada.

St Saviour's Church

Fosse Street

The Butterwalk

Royal Naval College

The Butterwalk Built 1635 to 1640. Its carved wooden fascia is supported on granite columns. Charles II held court in a room here while sheltering from storms in 1671. Now part of Dartmouth Museum.

The Boatfloat – an inner harbour accessible only to small craft

The Butterwalk

The Royal Naval College overlooking the town

The Cherub Inn in Higher Street – built in 1380, the town's oldest building

Cartoonist Simon Drew has been described as 'half artist, half wit'. His surreal drawings always raise a smile. He draws in his shop in Fosse Street and is usually happy to chat.

Lower Ferry slip
Bayard's Cove

The Embankment is a lovely uncluttered promenade, untainted by tourist tat. A railway station built near the Boatfleet has never seen a train, as plans for a rail bridge across the river couldn't be agreed on. The building is now an atmospheric restaurant.

Bayard's Cove, a cobbled quay lined with beautiful 18th-century houses, was where the Pilgrim Fathers put in when one of their two ships, *Speedwell*, sprung a leak. They sailed on to Plymouth where *Speedwell* was abandoned and the pilgrims all sailed on the other ship, the *Mayflower*, to America and into history. The quay is even more well-known to people of a certain age as a location for the 1970s TV drama, *The Onedin Line*.

A walk south to the mouth of the Dart takes you to Dartmouth Castle, the best-preserved of the two 15th-century fortifications on opposite sides of the river.

KINGSWEAR

Seen across the water from Dartmouth, with its pastel-coloured houses – once the homes of prosperous merchants and sea captains – stacked on a hill, Kingswear is an unforgettable sight. The attractive little town is the terminus for the Dartmouth Steam Railway, whose trains, in their distinctive yellow and brown livery, puff up and down the riverside. Kingswear also has a large marina with all the associated yards and services.

A ferry crossed the Dart as early as 1365; today there are three, saving around nine miles on a road journey between Paignton and Dartmouth via Totnes. At the Lower Ferry, a tug boat pushes and pulls a pontoon carrying up to eight cars and passengers across the river, while a nearby ferryboat connects steam railway passengers with Dartmouth waterfront. The Higher Ferry, just upstream, carries up to 36 cars, and runs on cables strung across the river.

The Lower Ferry at the Kingswear slip

Dartmouth Steam Railway terminus

Church of St Thomas of Canterbury
Site dates back to 1170 when Thomas Becket was murdered. The church was rebuilt in 1845-47 but the original 12th-century tower still stands

Passenger ferry jetty

The Royal Dart Inn

Lower Ferry slip

Kingswear from Dartmouth

RIVER DART

From sources high on Dartmoor, the River Dart meanders for around 30 miles through lovely countryside to its outlet at Dartmouth. The river is tidal below Totnes and there are no bridge crossings south of there, although Dartmouth has three ferry crossings. The Dart is one of the most famous salmon rivers in the southwest and during the build up to the 1944 Normandy invasion it was packed with landing craft and support ships. Villages along the river are well worth visiting, reached by driving along narrow minor roads.

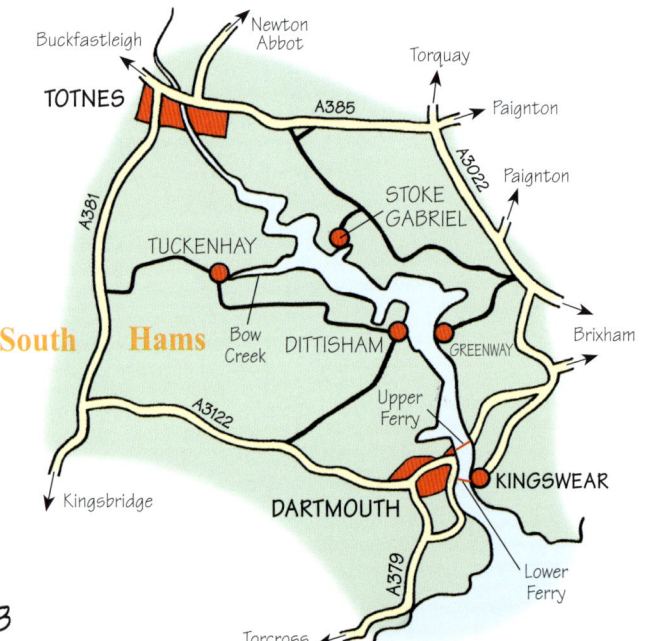

Dittisham

Dittisham, known locally as 'Ditsum', enjoys a sheltered location in a steep wooded valley running down to the river. Beautiful old paddle steamers once plied the Dart between Dartmouth and Totnes, and if a flag was raised, called at Dittisham Pier for passengers on the way. The famous plum crop and baskets of daffodils and snowdrops also travelled to Totnes market this way. The pier is now private and the pleasure boats no longer call. Dittisham has a couple of car parks but you have to walk to the riverside. The Ferry Boat Inn, wonderfully situated overlooking the river, is known as the FBI locally and boasts that it has not been 'subjected to an awful brewery facelift'.

Greenway House

The Greenway Ferry carries pedestrians across the river from Dittisham to the Greenway Estate. The imposing house, once the home of the crime writer Agatha Christie, is now owned by the National Trust and, with the gardens, open to the public.

The hamlet of Tuckenhay lies on secluded Bow Creek running west off the Dart, where barges and tall-masted ships once moored at the quayside. Tuckenhay Mill, now a holiday complex, used to produce hand-made paper of the finest quality for artists, banknotes and royal proclamations. The Maltsters Arms, an 18th-century riverside pub and restaurant, was once owned by the TV chef Keith Floyd.

The Maltsters Arms, Tuckenhay

Stoke Gabriel

When the tide goes out, reducing the Dart to a muddy stream, a weir at Stoke Gabriel retains a large mill pond which is a hugely popular place for children of all ages to catch crabs. The village has a timeless English quality with a gentle tangle of cottages leading down to the river and a 1,000 year old yew tree in the churchyard of St Mary & St Gabriel's Church, which has stood since Norman times. The Church House Inn was built in the 14th century to refresh the masons building the church. It, like the village, is unspoilt and friendly, with a fine medieval beam and plank ceiling, window seats and good ale. Oddities include an ancient mummified cat and old stocks outside that can still be used – so don't mess with the cat!

TOTNES

In 2007, *Time* magazine declared Totnes 'the capital of new age chic' and in 2008, *Highlife*, the British Airways magazine, declared it one of the world's 'Top 10 Funky Towns'. That may be a bit over the top but Totnes has certainly matured from a prosperous 16th-century port which exported cloth to France and brought back wine, to a laid-back market town which supports alternative lifestyles and antiquated hippies with a plethora of health food and vegetarian cafés.

In 2007, Totnes was the first place in Britain to introduce its own local alternative currency, the Totnes Pound. Shops in the town soon began accepting them as payment and giving them as change.

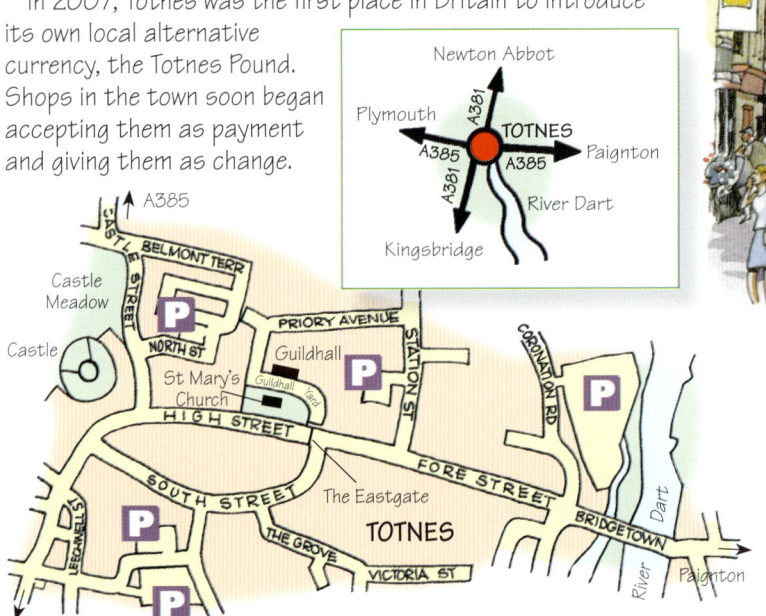

Fore Street

Most tourist interest centres on Fore Street and the High Street, which climb straight up the hill to the castle. A prominent feature of the town is the Eastgate, an arch spanning the middle of the main street. Originally the Elizabethan entrance to the walled town, it was rebuilt after being destroyed in a 1990 fire. The frequently crowded main streets are lined with 16th & 17th-century merchant's houses and a wealth of independent shops, with open market areas and pretty alleyways leading off to secluded courtyards.

The great sandstone tower of St Mary's Church dominates views of the town from the river. Close up, the 15th-century church building, backed by the Guildhall and the old town walls, is even more impressive.

Steamer Quay, at the bottom of the town, still caters for working river boats, and pleasure trips regularly arrive upstream from Dartmouth – one of the finest approaches to the town.

You can also arrive, or leave, on the South Devon Railway. Steam trains travel daily during the summer along the Dart Valley between Buckfastleigh and Littlehampton stations.

High Street

Overhung building at the top of High Street – and a hippie

Totnes Castle is a perfect example of a small Norman motte and bailey fortress. Set in pleasant parkland, it's remarkable well preserved and a great viewpoint over the town and river.

Ramparts Walk, under the Eastgate, leads to Guildhall Yard and the ancient Guildhall, where there's an old jail and a table that Oliver Cromwell sat at in 1646. Remarkably, the town council still meets in the building.

The bridge over the River Dart

DARTMOOR

Southern England's largest expanse of wilderness, Dartmoor's 365 square miles encompasses granite uplands rising to over 2,000ft (610m), bogs, grassland, dense woods, heather-strewn moorland, and rolling green hills dotted with grazing sheep and cows. The entire area is also rich in antiquities and archaeology.

Many of Devon's rivers have a catchment area on the Moor. As well as helping to shape the landscape, they have traditionally provided a source of power for industries such as tin mining and quarrying.

Walking is one of the main moorland activities, from short jaunts to challenging treks across isolated uplands. The Moor also has a reputation for dampness with its mists attaining legendary status. Setting out on a walk in unpredictable weather should never be attempted without proper preparation.

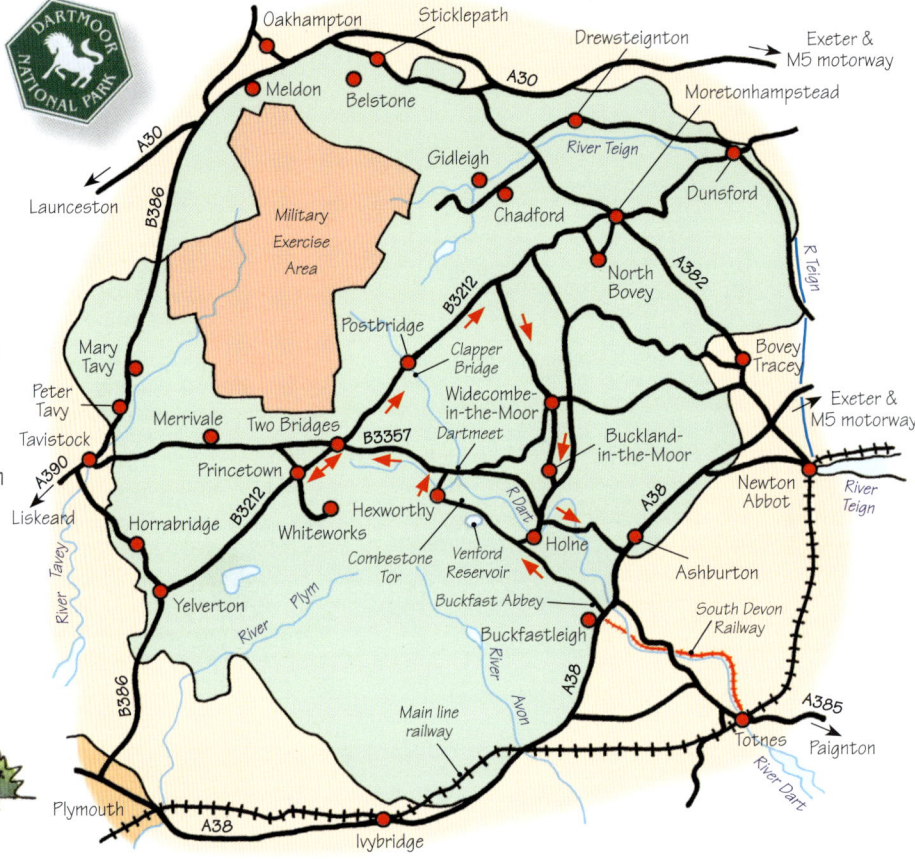

High Moorland Visitor Centre at Princetown
Sir Arthur Conan Doyle started to write 'The Hound of the Baskervilles' here when the building was The Duchy Hotel.

DARTMOOR TOUR

A circular drive of around 30 miles is an excellent way to sample the amazing variety of landscapes that this remarkable part of Devon has to offer.

Beginning at Buckfastleigh, take in Buckfast Abbey, then travel on country roads past Venford Reservoir to Hexworthy and a possible diversion to Dartmeet, a lovely beauty spot on the river. Visit Two Bridges and Princetown, before returning along the B3212 to see the clapper bridge at Postbridge. Continue for around four miles across the loneliest part of the Moor, then turn off the main road for Widecombe-in-the-Moor and Buckland-in-the-Moor. Country roads, winding through attractive countryside, take you to Ashburton and the A38 return to Buckfastleigh. You'll need a spirit of adventure and a good road map. Enjoy!

There's a speed limit of 40 miles per hour throughout the Moor. Some roads are narrow and only suitable for cars and small vehicles. Look out for the famous ponies which roam unrestricted and will cross roads without looking. Take care and do not feed them.

Free car parks and lay-bys are helpfully positioned at some of the best viewpoints on the moor. If you see a car park or a lay-by you can be sure there's something worthwhile to stop for.

Buckfast Abbey

The centre-piece of a living monastic community, the magnificent Abbey Church was restored by just six monks – only one of them who had masonry experience.

The original monastery, established here in 1018, fell into disrepair during the 1536-40 Dissolution until restoration began in 1907 and was completed in 1937.

Princetown

At 1,300ft (397m), Princetown is the highest small town on the Moor. Dominated by its notorious jail since 1805, when prisoners from the American War of Independence and Naploneonic Wars were held there, it once housed over 6,000 prisoners and currently holds around 600 category C inmates. Famous detainees have included Frank 'the Mad Axeman' Mitchell, whom the Kray brothers helped to escape, and the Irish Republicans Michael Davitt and Eamon de Valera, who went on to become Prime Minister and President of the Irish Republic. The prison is scheduled for closure, but at an undecided date.

Other Princetown attractions include the High Moorland Visitor Centre and the Prison Museum.

Dartmoor Prison

The B3357 road bridge over the West Dart

The bridge to the hotel car park

Dartmoor is known for its **tors** – hills topped with outcrops of bedrock, which in granite country such as this are usually rounded boulder-like formations. More than 160 Dartmoor hills have the word tor in their name.

Two Bridges
Generally reckoned to be the centre point of Dartmoor, the tiny settlement of Two Bridges is set where the West Dart and Cowsick rivers converge, with a famous hostelry where Vivian Leigh once stayed, and – yes! – two ancient bridges. The Two Bridges Hotel replaced the Saracen's Head, which had been used as a vegetable market. To celebrate the new building in 1902, Eden Philpotts, a friend of Agatha Christie, wrote *The River*, one of his 18 books set on the Moor.

Combestone Tor

Postbridge
A rather nondescript hamlet but a good walking centre, best known for its 13th-century clapper bridge, the largest and best preserved of the Dartmoor stone bridges. First used by medieval tin-miners and farmers, these simple structures consist of huge slabs of granite supported by piers of the same material.

There's the remains of an even higher clapper bridge at **Dartmeet**, a popular beauty spot set in a steep wooded valley on the B3357, where the East and West Dart meet in a chaos of boulders and white water. A large car park is to hand with a nearby ice cream shop and a tea garden just up-river. The scenery is magnificent and a short walk up the valley soon leaves the crowds behind.

The clapper bridge and the road bridge at Postbridge

Widecombe-in-the-Moor

Buckland-in-the-Moor
One of the cluster of moorstone and thatch hamlets on the eastern side of Dartmoor, surrounded by open moorland but enveloped in thick woodland in the winding Webburn Valley. The clock on the castellated tower of the 14th-century church of St Peter has the words 'my dear mother' replacing the numbers. It was a gift to the parish from the Lord of the Manor William Whitney in 1939. Though pretty, Buckland is too scattered to be memorable, but the cluster of thatched cottages at the east side of the village can stop you in your tracks.

Widecombe-in-the-Moor
The small but most-visited and probably most-famous of all the Dartmoor villages with the coach park to prove it. Widecombe Fair has become more of a gymkhana these days rather than the market it was when the popular song was first written down in 1880 and 'Bill Brewer, Jan Stewer, Peter Gurney, Peter Davy Dan'l Whiddon, Harry Hawk, and Old Uncle Tom Cobley and all' attended. Tom Pearce's grey mare died after someone borrowed it to go to the fair, but the song accuses none of the above.

Dubbed 'The Cathedral of the Moor', St Pancras Church is a lofty landmark from miles around. It's 120ft (37m) tower, funded by 16th-century tinners, dwarfs the 14th-century nave beneath.

Buckland-in-the-Moor

Torcross, Slapton Ley and Slapton Sands

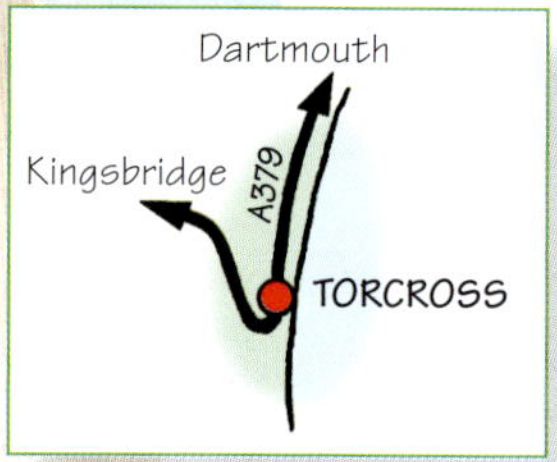

TORCROSS

A small, exposed village with pubs, shops, tea rooms and cottages, Torcross lies at the southern end of Slapton Sands, a three-mile stretch of shingle beach. Though protected by a sea wall, the village is periodically battered by fierce winter gales, with waves and pebbles being flung over the buildings into the lake beyond.

It's an unusual, rugged kind of a place, far from the south Devon chocolate-box stereotype, but still full of interest. There's also sadness when you walk along that great swath of shingle, thrown up when the glaciers melted after the last Ice Age, and consider the tragic events that occurred here in 1944.

Devon's largest freshwater lake, Slapton Ley, occupies the landward side of the road along the beach. It's a National Nature Reserve and Site of Special Scientific Interest, noted for its wildfowl and wildlife.

Pilchard's Cove, near the hamlet of Strete, is a long-established naturist beach. However, recent landslips now restrict access, so the hardy visitors now use the northern end of Slapton Sands.

SLAPTON SANDS

The Sherman tank memorial

As it's predominately shingle, Slapton Sands is a misleading name. The American military used the straight, three-mile beach for the ill-fated Exercise Tiger in preparation for the D-Day landings in 1944.

During exercises a tragic series of events led to the loss of 946 American lives in what has since been called one of the great tragedies of World War Two. It was also one of the military's best kept secrets until revealed to the world 40 years later through the efforts of a local hotelier, Ken Small.

As live ammunition was to be used in the exercises, 3,000 people and their animals were ordered to leave their homes. Villages around Slapton were deserted. The scale and trauma of the evacuation are memorably evoked by Leslie Thomas in his 1981 novel, *The Magic Army*.

It's thought that the first deaths occurred during a friendly fire incident. Next day, due to a mix-up with communications and lack of escort vessels, the Royal Navy off-shore defences were breached and nine German torpedo boats sunk three American assault ships with heavy casualties.

An American Sherman tank on the sands car park is their memorial. Lost from a landing craft during the tragedy, the tank was salvaged from 65ft (20m) of water in 1984, thanks again to the remarkable Ken Small, which was acknowledged by President Reagan in a personal letter. Ken died in 2004 and the tank is his memorial also.

BLACKPOOL SANDS

A beautiful crescent of golden shingle, just along the coast from Slapton, Blackpool Sands slopes down to a turquoise blue sea, sheltered by green fields, magnificent pine trees and craggy cliffs. It's frequently voted South Devon's favourite beach. A car park, cafe and facilities are discretely hidden amongst the trees.

Blackpool Sands

SALCOMBE

Situated at the seaward end of the Kingsbridge estuary, Salcombe is sailing heaven. Everything here seems to revolve around boats. Once Salcombe Bay was busy with fleets of clippers and schooners bringing fresh fruit from The West Indies, now it's all manner of small sailing craft that cram the broad waterway. Seen from the steep hillside across the Salcombe rooftops, twinkling in the sunshine and with a backdrop of the rolling hills of the South Hams, it's one of south Devon's greatest sights. The Kingsbridge Estuary runs inland for some five miles with numerous side channels. The 'estuary' is actually a ria or drowned valley caused by rising sea levels rather than a true estuary and its size is way out of proportion to the few rivers that discharge into it.

The Salcombe Formerly The Salcombe Hotel. Now apartments

Ferry Boat Inn

Salcombe to East Portlemouth ferry landing

Rising from the long waterfront, pastel coloured villas and terraces rise attractively up the steep hillside. Many are second homes with affluent owners and it's said that during the summer the population increases tenfold and Salcombe becomes Chelsea-on-Sea. The town has the second-highest property prices in the UK outside of central London – after Sandbanks, Poole.

Many of the shops, bars and restaurants in the town, especially around Fore Street, cater for a predominantly well-off, fashionable and nautically-inclined clientele, with prices to match. Despite that, and possibly because of it, the town has an amiable, easygoing confidence that's much appreciated by its less well-heeled visitors.

The narrow main street runs parallel with the waterside, usually busy with pedestrians and motorists vainly looking for somewhere to park and wondering how they are going to exit the single road. Parking in Salcombe is difficult. The largest car park is in Gould Road but the centre of town is a good walk from there. Day visitors can use the park and drive system from the town outskirts in summer. The grandest way to arrive is on a ferry from Kingsbridge. It's an enjoyable trip and the view of Salcombe from the water is sensational.

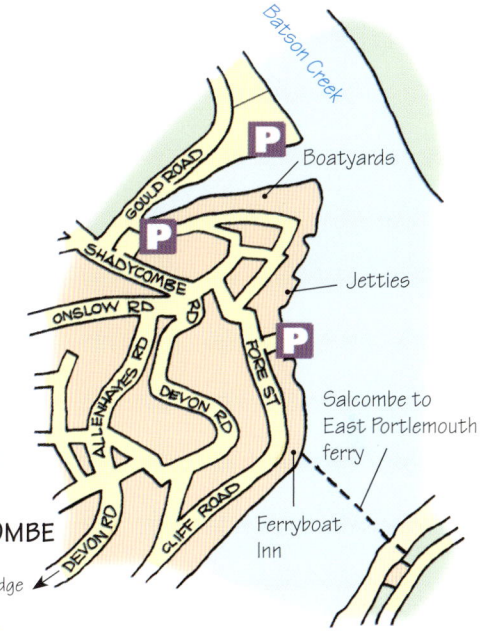

Holy Trinity Church

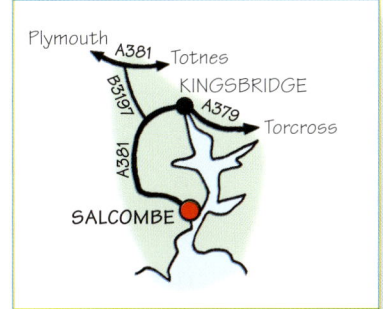

The East Portlemouth ferry crosses the estuary to a long and sandy beach that curls delightfully towards the open sea. The ferry leaves from the appropriately named and pleasingly underdeveloped Ferry Boat Inn. To relax in its sunny garden, glass in hand, while watching the boats glide by and chatting to a couple of London stockbrokers, is to sample the essence of Salcombe's many charms.

The Salcombe to East Portlemouth Ferry – with canine crew

South Sands Ferry

A cheery ferry chugs up and down the estuary to and from a tiny golden beach at North Sands near the picturesque ruin of Salcombe Castle. Built as protection against French & Spanish raiders in 1544, the fortification fell to English hands during the Civil War.

South Sands and Splat Cove are also worth exploring. This lovely area is surrounded by high, tree-clad cliffs that leave barely enough room for the tiny beaches. Be careful not to over-relax and doze off on the beach, as some of them disappear at high tide!

Salcombe Bay from Devon Road

PRAWLE POINT

The southernmost point of Devon, Prawle Point, was once a hangout for 16th-century pirates and more recently notorious for its dense fogs and the resultant shipwrecks. A lighthouse, built in 1836 and still operational, has made Start Bay considerably safer for shipping.

Except for walkers on the South West Coast Path, this part of the South Hams, crisscrossed by minor roads, is off the usual tourist trail but has a timeless charm that's worthwhile exploring.

Linger awhile at the tranquil village of East Prawle where the delightfully named Pig's Nose Inn is packed with rustic paraphernalia, presided over by former music manager Peter Webber, who occasionally disturbs the rural peace by persuading big name bands to gig at the 16th-century inn.

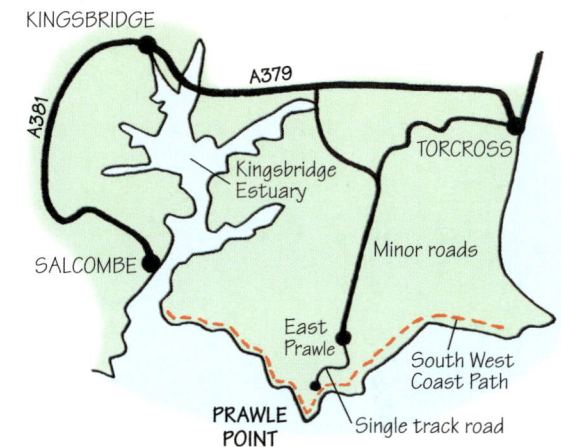

A single track road from East Prawle takes you to a small National Trust car park near the lighthouse. The views from the point across Start Bay to the River Dart are wonderfully extensive. Provided of course, it's not foggy.

Prawle Point

KINGSBRIDGE

A transport hub at the head of the estuary, Kingsbridge has been known as 'the capital of South Hams' since the 13th century. With some fine Tudor and Georgian buildings along an accessible main street, a variety of good independent shops, a constant resident population and ample car parking, the cheerful market town is almost the antithesis of its more glamourous neighbour (Salcombe) five miles down the estuary.

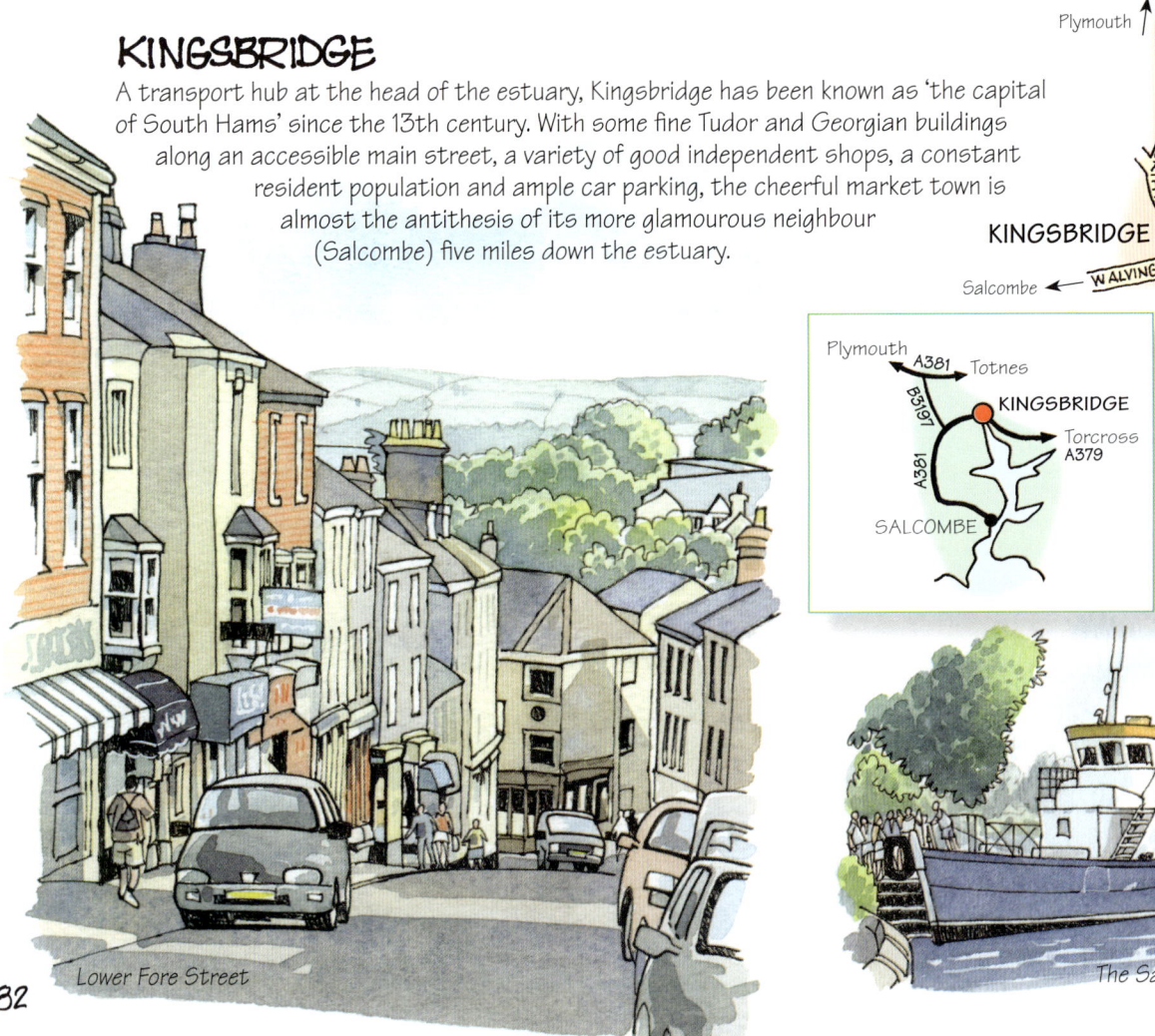

Lower Fore Street

The Salcombe to Kingsbridge ferry

St Edmunds King & Martyr Church consecrated in 1414, has a 150 year-old organ and a peal of eight bells

The **town hall clock** has only three faces. The fourth faces the site of a 19th-century workhouse and, as legend has it, was left blank to prevent the inmates clockwatching

The former town hall

The former town hall and Reel Cinema

The Shambles

The Kingsbridge Cookworthy Museum

Fore Street

Relative normality can be deceptive and Kingsbridge has some interesting oddities to delight the discerning visitor. Pretty alleys off Fore Street can lead to surprising places and a walk up Fore Street passing old 18th- and 19th-century merchants' houses keeps the head turning.

The former town hall now houses a country market and the independent, family run, Reel Cinema. Most surprising is the huge Toy Town clock which adorns the roof. The Shambles, or market arcade, next door was rebuilt in 1796 but retains its 16th-century granite pillars. Further up the hill a grammar school, dating back to 1670, now houses the Kingsbridge Cookworthy Museum, devoted to the 18th-century discoverer of English china clay, and producer of the first English porcelain, William Cookworthy, who was born in the town.

HOPE COVE

With safe and sandy beaches, rock pools, a pub, restaurant, village shop and car park, all cradled in a dramatic double sweep of jagged cliffs, Hope Cove is a Mecca for the family bucket and spade brigade.

Historically, the village falls into two parts – Outer Hope and Inner Hope. Inner Hope fell within the parish of Malborough until the 1970s, when it was united with its neighbour on the other side of a small headland. Once a remote village, Hope developed as a centre for the local fishing industry with a sideline of smuggling and plundering wrecked ships.

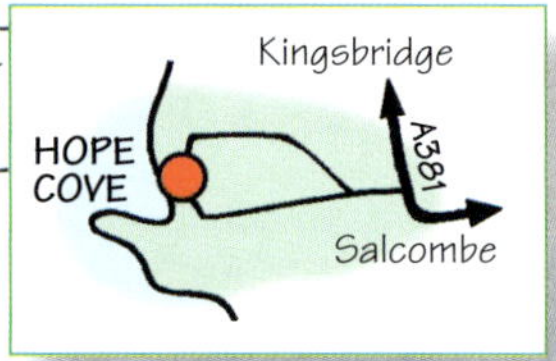

One of the ships of the Spanish Armada, St. Peter the Great, was wrecked on Shippen Rock in 1588. The Village Inn at Thurlestone and a number of other South Hams' buildings are said to incorporate beams salvaged from the wreckage.

Inner Hope

Thatched cottage at Outer Hope

Outer Hope beach

Inner Hope beach

The Hope & Anchor pub and the village shop are located in Outer Hope, making it the centre for village and beach life. It gets crowded but like many small holiday hotspots the number of visitors is 'controlled' by the number of spaces in the car park. When that's full, so is the village. Get there early.

A narrow road runs past a row of cottages and a neat village green to Inner Hope, the quieter cove, where boats are launched and the remnants of the once large fishing fleet still land lobsters and crabs. Pots, floats, rope and all the paraphernalia of fishing are scattered picturesquely around, appropriately overlooked by the Hope Cove Gallery, located in a former fisherman's store.

THURLESTONE

With thatched cottages at the landward end and a modern estate of upmarket mansions overlooking Bigbury Bay at the other, Thurlestone is a village of contrasts. Small estates adjoin the single leafy street and a church, village shop and The Village Inn pub gather picturesquely around a small green. Peaceful and pleasant enough, but it's the beaches and golf course that draw the crowds here.

The single road swings left at the church and leaves the village behind. A short walk from the car park by the golf club takes you to Thurlestone Sands, a beach highly rated for its water quality and surfing.

A striking rock archway lies just off the beach to which the village owes its name: Thurlestone means 'holed rock' in old English.

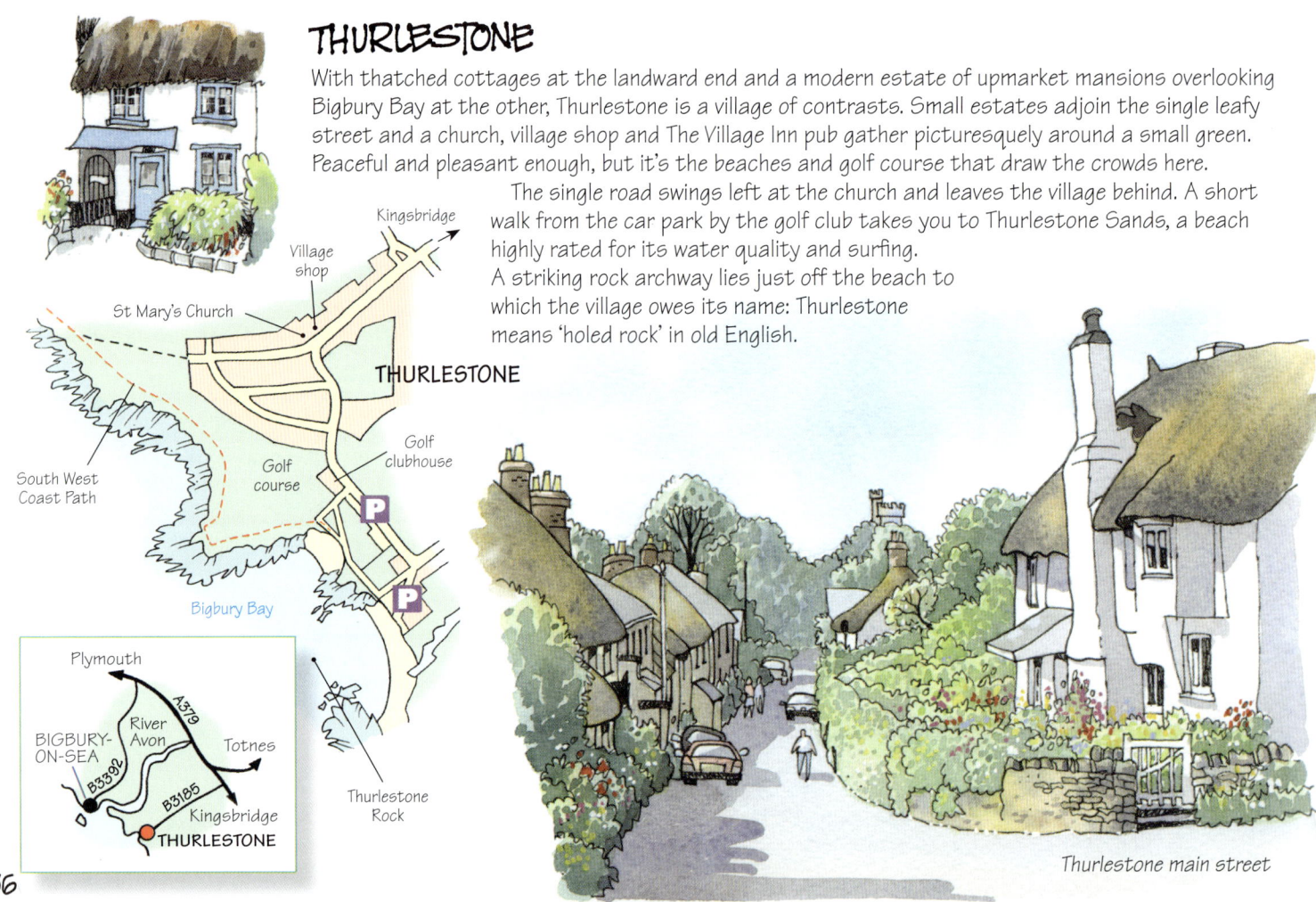

Thurlestone main street

St Mary's Church and the village shop

Thurlestone Rock

A pathway from the 13th-century All Saints Church leads to a road through a fabulous estate of exclusive homes to an equally fabulous cliff-top golf course, described by Peter Allis as 'one of the most beautiful courses in the South West of England – reminiscent of Pebble Beach, USA'. A public footpath across the lush greens joins the coast path. Head north and the view, already wide and airy, opens up to a fantastic panorama across the bay to Bigbury-on-Sea, the River Avon estuary and Burgh Island. Take a picnic, you won't want to leave (see page 88).

Thurlestone Rock

The golf course

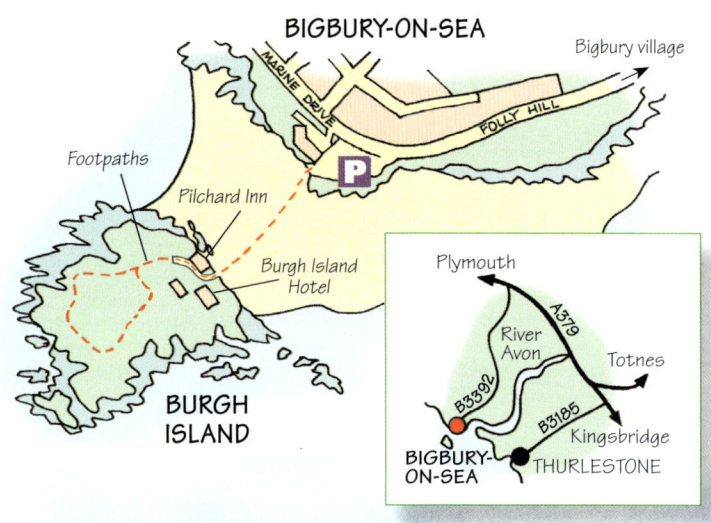

BIGBURY-ON-SEA

From a few fishermen's cottages at the start of the 20th century, Bigbury-on-Sea has mushroomed into a vibrant holiday centre with a post office and stores, two cafés and the Burgh Island Causeway resort, built in 1998 to replace the burnt-out Tom Crocker pub.

A wonderful open, sandy beach, the largest in south Devon, curves around the village at the mouth of the Devon Avon. The beach was sold at auction in May 2013 for £70,000, with the new owner promising there would be no new development.

Burgh Island rises dramatically some 270yds (250m) offshore. Technically only an island at high tide, you can walk to it along a sandy causeway when the tide is out. There are several buildings on the grass-topped, rocky outcrop: the Burgh Island Hotel, three private houses and a pub, the Pilchard Inn, run by the hotel.

Bigbury Bay from the coast path

The sea tractor

The causeway and Burgh Island

The hotel operates a sea tractor, transporting passengers back and forth when the tide covers the causeway. The original was constructed in 1930 with the current, third generation model dating from 1969. The tractor drives across the beach with its wheels underwater on the sandy bottom while its driver and passengers sit on a platform high above. Hydraulic motors relay power from a Fordson tractor engine to the wheels. This wonderful contrivance can operate in 10ft (3.5m) of water and cope with seas up to a force nine gale.

Burgh Island Hotel was described in the 1930s as 'the smartest hotel west of the Ritz' with aristocrats, royals and showbiz celebrities streaming through its elegant doors. After a post-war decline the hotel was rescued in the 1980s and its glamour restored. An eccentric millionaire, Archibald Hettlefold, owned the island and commissioned the original Art Deco style building in 1929, as a guest house for his friends.

The Pilchard Inn

PLYMOUTH

Devon's largest city and home to around 250,000 people, Plymouth is completely different from anywhere else in the county. The River Tamar, the border with neighbouring Cornwall, flows into the immense Plymouth Sound which for centuries has been a vital part of the South Coast's maritime history.

Plymouth was heavily bombed by the Luftwaffe during World War Two. Although the dockyards were the principal target, most of the city centre was destroyed and more than 1,000 civilians lost their lives. Miraculously, much of the old harbour area survived and, now known as the Barbican, its ancient streets and historical sites make it an evocative place to visit.

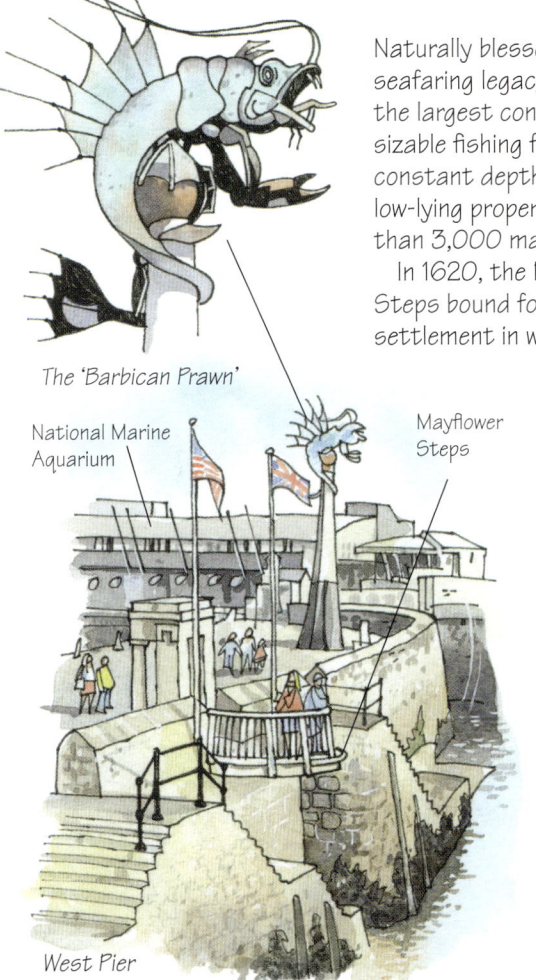

The 'Barbican Prawn'

National Marine Aquarium

Mayflower Steps

West Pier

Naturally blessed with one of Europe's finest deep-water anchorages, Plymouth has a legendry seafaring legacy. The early port settlement, now the Barbican, has around 100 listed buildings and the largest concentration of cobbled streets in Britain, with New Street the oldest in the city. A sizable fishing fleet still docks in Sutton Harbour, which was enclosed by a lock in 1993 to provide a constant depth of water for fishing and pleasure craft, and to reduce the risk of flood damage to low-lying properties. The nearby National Marine Aquarium is Britain's largest aquarium with more than 3,000 marine animals on display.

In 1620, the Pilgrim Fathers set sail on the Mayflower from near the commemorative Mayflower Steps bound for the New World where they established the Plymouth Colony – the second English settlement in what is now the United States of America.

The 'Barbican Prawn', officially called 'The Plymouth Sea Monster,' was erected in 1996, designed by Brian Fell of Glossop, Darbyshire. The sculpture, in a variety of metallic materials, stands 33ft (10m) above the West Pier and represents the diversity of fish and shellfish landed on the Barbican. Though greeted with derision when first erected, it's now been accepted, like many of the odd-looking statues and buildings in the area, as part of the Barbican's collection of curios.

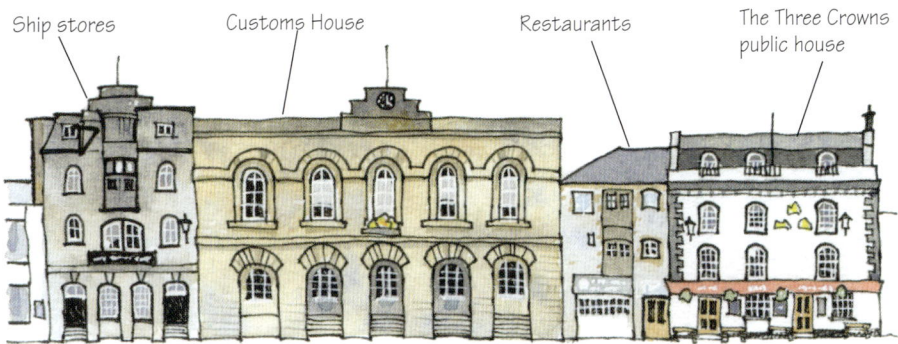

Ship stores | Customs House | Restaurants | The Three Crowns public house

An eclectic mix of buildings along the north side of The Parade

Plymouth Hoe, a broad and breezy hilltop swath of grass, dotted with monuments is perhaps best known for the probably apocryphal story that Sir Francis Drake played his famous game of bowls here in 1588 while waiting for the tide to change before joining the English fleet to defeat the Spanish Armada. More recently, in 1966, Sir Francis Chichester stepped ashore at West Hoe pier after his epic solo circumnavigation of the world aboard Gypsy Moth IV.

The city boasts over twenty war memorials, nine of which are on the Hoe. The largest, the Plymouth Naval Memorial, commemorates the Royal Navy personnel killed in the two World Wars. A statue of Drake by Joseph Boehm, a copy of the original in his home town of Tavistock, was placed here during 1884 in his honour.

A broad tarmac promenade across the hilltop serves as a spectacular military parade ground and a site for funfairs and open-air concerts. The Hoe is also a terrific grandstand for the famous British Firework Championships, held over two days in August. Tinside Lido, built by the local unemployed to keep them busy during the Depression, sits on the limestone waterside. The elegant seawater pool has been recently restored to its 1930s jazz age glory. Nearby, the Belvedere, a three-tiered bandstand known locally as the wedding cake, is a good place to sit and enjoy the sea views.

Sir Francis Drake statue

The Plymouth Dome restaurant & bar

Smeaton's Tower

Drake Statue

Naval Memorial

Plymouth Hoe

Tinside Lido

Warships in the Sound

The iconic red and white bands of Smeaton's Tower demand attention. Designed by civil engineer John Smeaton, this was once the top section of Eddystone Lighthouse, built some 14 miles out to sea in 1759. When replaced in 1882, the lighthouse was dismantled stone by stone and this part reassembled on the Hoe. A steep climb up 93 steps inside is rewarded by sensational views from its lantern room, some 90ft (27m) above the ground.

   The Royal Citadel was built between the Hoe and Sutton Harbour in the 1660s, both to protect the port and probably also to intimidate the townsfolk who had leaned towards Parliament during the Civil War. The massive, star-shaped stone fortress remains occupied by the military and still looks pretty scary.

   There's always a great deal of activity on the water, including frequent warship movements, ferry traffic with France and Spain, fishing trawlers and a swarm of sailing craft, large and small. The annual Fastnet yacht race also ends here.

   Postwar, Devonport Dockyard was kept busy refitting aircraft carriers such as the Ark Royal and later, nuclear submarines, while new light industry factories were constructed in the newly-zoned industrial sector, attracting rapid growth of the urban population. Industries may come and go but the view from the Hoe of the Sound to Drake's Island remains one of the most evocative maritime landscapes in Britain.

Smeaton's Tower

AUTHOR'S NOTES

Geography
The county of Devon (also known historically, as Devonshire), covers 2,590 square miles with a population of around 1.1 million. It's bordered by Cornwall to the west, Somerset to the northeast and Dorset to the southeast. Devon is the only county in England to have two separate stretches of coastline, with the Bristol Channel in the north and the English Channel in the south. Both coastlines have cliffs and sandy shores, with the bays containing seaside resorts, fishing towns and ports.

Inland, the terrain is generally rural and hilly with a low population density compared to other parts of England. Devon has more miles of roads than any other county in the country.

The high moorland of Dartmoor consists of granite rock. Much of the remainder of the county is sandstone and shales, with the South Hams made up of slate, sandstone and volcanic rocks. The red rocks of the Triassic geological period feature in east Devon with a complicated geological combination including pebble beds, sandstones, and mudstones. Around Sidmouth Greensand turns the cliffs grey.

Rock formation at Prawle Point

Thatched cottage at Northlew

Thatched Cottages
A Devon thatched cottage with a colourful country garden has featured on so many boxes of chocolates it has acquired the modern appellation 'chocolate box' as a derisory term. Thatching is employed in developing countries using low-cost, local vegetation but in the developed world it's often the choice of affluent folk who like a rustic look for their home.

Most thatch in the West Country is straw, which generally does not require frequent maintenance and will normally last for 15-25 years, although re-ridging will need to done after 10-15 years. Despite the perceived fire risk (thatch actually burns slowly, like a 'closed book') there are about 60,000 thatched roofs in the UK and more are being built each year, employing approximately 1,000 full-time thatchers.

Old thatched buildings often have walls of cob, a mixture of clay, sand and water, traditionally trampled by oxen. Walls are generally around 24in (60cm) thick with small, deep-set windows, giving thatched cottages a rather mysterious appearance, beloved of children's fairy tales.

Clotted Cream
Produced from milk with the highest fat content. This is left to stand in a pan for between 12 and 24 hours, then gently heated – not boiled – until a solid ring of clotted cream forms around the edge. The pan is then left covered in a cool place for another 24 hours before the cream is skimmed off with a slotted spoon. Clotted cream is one of the main ingredients of a West Country cream tea, a culinary treat that no visitor to Devon should ever miss.

Scrumpy (Devon cider)
Originally produced on farms from their own orchards and intended only for consumption by family, friends and labourers, whose wages were often paid partly in cider. Traditionally it's made from two varieties of apple, bittersharps and bittersweets, which are milled together, made into a 'cheese' layered with straw or cloth and pressed. The juice is collected in barrels and allowed to ferment naturally. The resultant blend varies considerably in taste between sweet and dry, but the strength of any scrumpy should never be underestimated!

Dartmouth

Also in the Sketchbook series...

Jim Watson was born and bred in the English Lake District and moved to Rugby at the age of 18 to take up an engineering apprenticeship. He worked as a draughtsman for a while before leaving secure employment to pursue a freelance career drawing kid's comics. Since then, Jim has produced a wide range of cartoon and illustrative work for magazines and books. He has written and illustrated 16 books of his own. This is his seventh for Survival Books.

The Sketchbook series of books, written and illustrated by Jim Watson, are packed with his evocative line and watercolour illustrations. Each book features around 40 favourite locations and tells you how to drive there, where to park and what to look out for. With history, facts and figures, they are the perfect companions to guide you to new places and remember old favourites. The books have colour throughout their 96 pages and are beautifully bound in hard back, making them ideal for gifts.

Lake District Sketchbook   ISBN 9781907339097   £9.95
Cotswold Sketchbook   ISBN 9781907339103   £9.95
London Sketchbook   ISBN 9781907339370   £10.95
Cornwall Sketchbook   ISBN 9781907339417   £10.95

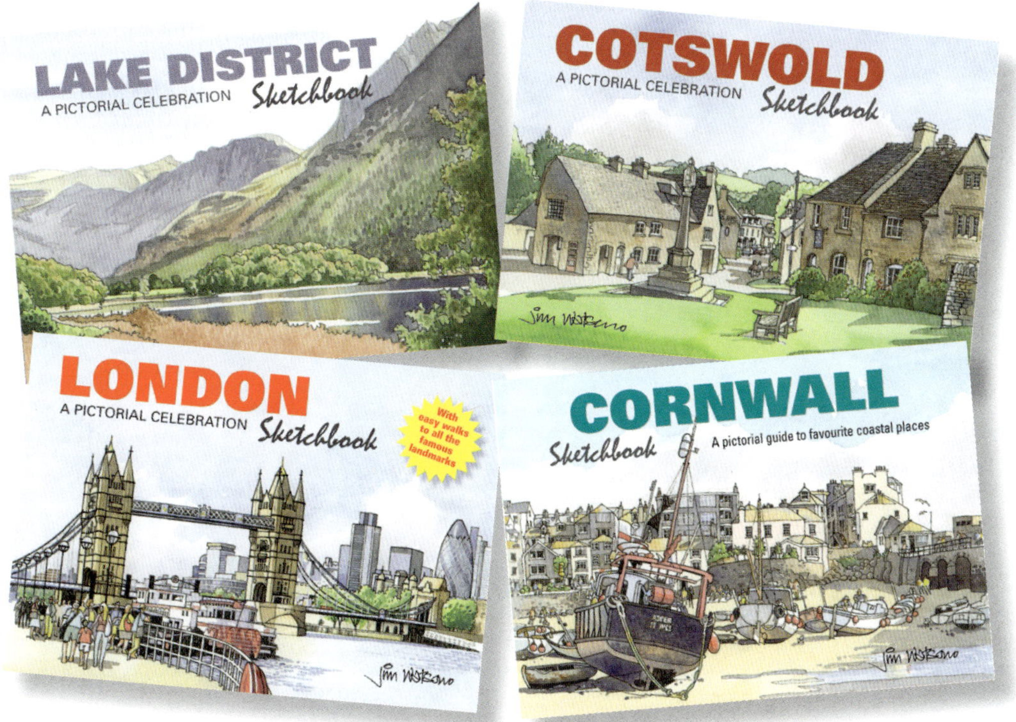

Celebrating Britain's most popular tourist destinations

Survival Books • www.survivalbooks.net